Cambridge Elements ≡

Elements in the Problems of God
edited by
Michael L. Peterson
Asbury Theological Seminary

CATHOLICISM AND THE PROBLEM OF GOD

Mark K. Spencer
University of St. Thomas

CAMBRIDGE
UNIVERSITY PRESS

Shaftesbury Road, Cambridge CB2 8EA, United Kingdom

One Liberty Plaza, 20th Floor, New York, NY 10006, USA

477 Williamstown Road, Port Melbourne, VIC 3207, Australia

314–321, 3rd Floor, Plot 3, Splendor Forum, Jasola District Centre, New Delhi – 110025, India

103 Penang Road, #05–06/07, Visioncrest Commercial, Singapore 238467

Cambridge University Press is part of Cambridge University Press & Assessment, a department of the University of Cambridge.

We share the University's mission to contribute to society through the pursuit of education, learning and research at the highest international levels of excellence.

www.cambridge.org
Information on this title: www.cambridge.org/9781009467919

DOI: 10.1017/9781009290661

First published 2023

A catalogue record for this publication is available from the British Library

ISBN 978-1-009-46791-9 Hardback
ISBN 978-1-009-29067-8 Paperback
ISSN 2754-8724 (online)
ISSN 2754-8716 (print)

Catholicism and the Problem of God

Elements in the Problems of God

DOI: 10.1017/9781009290661
First published online: October 2023

Mark K. Spencer
University of St. Thomas

Author for correspondence: Mark K. Spencer, spen8444@stthomas.edu

Abstract: This Element is an overview of the Catholic conception of God and of philosophical problems regarding God that arose during its historical development. After summarizing key Catholic doctrines, Section 1 considers problems regarding God that arose because Catholicism originally drew on both Jewish and Greek conceptions of God. Section 2 turns to controversies regarding God as Trinitarian and incarnate, which arose in early church councils, with reference to how that conception developed during the Middle Ages. In Section 3, the author considers problems regarding God's actions toward creatures, including creation, providence, predestination, and the nature of divine action in itself. Finally, Section 4 considers problems regarding how we relate to God. The Element focuses on tensions among different Catholic spiritualities, and on problems having to do with analogical language about God and human desire for God.

Keywords: Catholicism, God, Trinity, incarnation, spirituality

ISBNs: 9781009467919 (HB), 9781009290678 (PB), 9781009290661 (OC)
ISSNs: 2754-8724 (online), 2754-8716 (print)

Contents

1 The Basic Catholic Conception of God and Its Jewish and Greek Inheritance

This Element presents an overview of Catholicism's conception of God and of philosophical debates that arose as it developed. While I consider these debates in historical order, this Element is not a work of history or textual interpretation, and I mostly focus on issues internal to Catholicism. I begin with problems generated by Catholicism's origins. The Catholic Church understands itself to have been founded by Jesus Christ, held to be God incarnate, God's definitive revelation, who by dying on the Cross and rising from the dead revealed God's self-giving love and united humanity to God. Its conception of God is an unpacking of that revelation (CCC nos. 65–7, 813–16). To understand how that revelation was experienced, thinkers in the Catholic tradition drew on the conception of God in the Hebrew Scriptures and on Jewish practices because Catholics understood Christ and the Catholic Church to fulfill the ancient religion of Israel. Catholicism also developed in the Hellenistic world and drew upon Greek philosophical and cultural conceptions of the divine.

In this section, after presenting some core Catholic doctrines, I consider how this dual inheritance undergirds Catholicism's conception of God and how it led to problems about God. In Section 2, I consider how the first seven ecumenical councils (meetings of bishops that officially settled questions of doctrine) developed a conception of God as Trinitarian and incarnate. Section 3 considers how Catholics have understood God's relations to creatures, especially human persons; I focus on medieval debates about providence, predestination, and divine action. Finally, in Section 4, I consider how differing accounts of how human persons relate to God affect how God is conceived. Here, I focus on philosophical problems generated by differing approaches to Catholic spiritual practices and the question of how we know and desire God.

1.1 Catholic Sources and Doctrines

The Catholic Church conceives of God as three persons, who take initiative in relating to us; Catholicism's conception of God is meant to facilitate our relating to God in return (Benedict XVI 2005: 1). God's self-revelation includes propositions about himself, and we can formulate true propositions describing what and who God is (*ST* I q.13). In this Element, I consider Catholic conceptions of God, in the sense of both how God has been described in official doctrine and how God is understood in various Catholic theologies and spiritualities. Tensions among these conceptions, which influence Catholic experiences of God, give rise to philosophical problems.

In unpacking the revelation of God in the life, death, resurrection, and ascension of Jesus Christ, the Catholic Church primarily draws on Scripture (the Old Testament or Hebrew Scriptures and the New Testament) and a broader tradition of teachings. The conception of God that results from that unpacking is found in several sources. To get the fullest sense of how Catholic tradition conceives of God and inculcates that conception in Catholics, one should look to the texts and rituals of the Church's liturgies (Fagerberg 2021). If one wishes to find propositional formulations of the core aspects of the Catholic conception of God, one should look to definitive or "magisterial" teachings by bishops (leaders of the Church in a local area, who are understood to be successors of the Apostles, the earliest followers of Christ) and the Pope (the bishop of Rome, understood to be the successor of St. Peter, the leader of the Apostles). This official teaching, which all Catholics are obliged to believe, is found in councils of the whole Church, in the collective teaching of the bishops, and in solemn teachings by the Pope. Christ is understood to have given teaching authority to the Apostles, which was passed on to their successors. The tradition's content is also found in the teachings of theologians, especially those known as the Fathers and Doctors of the Church; the former are those from the earliest centuries of the Church whose thought forms the theological basis for Catholic teachings and practices, while the latter are those from throughout Church history whose thought has decisively influenced Catholic understanding. Theologians drew upon many non-Catholic philosophical and cultural traditions about God, and so aspects of those traditions have also entered Catholic conceptions of God (Cano 1563; Newman 1994; D 1507, 4150, 4202–14; Joy 2017). Catholics' conceptions of God are also based on the saints, those who most lived like Christ and are now deemed worthy of veneration and emulation, because, in them, God's life and influence are distinctively displayed (Balthasar 2009: 529–41). Finally, the content of tradition and of the Catholic conception of God is found in the "sense of all the faithful" for what has been believed "always, everywhere, and by all" (Vincent of Lerins, developed by Newman 1994; D 4161), some of which is embodied in popular devotions. Still, what counts as tradition, magisterial teaching, or the sense of the faithful, and what the tradition means, is subject to interpretation and debate.

On the Catholic view, one *perceives* the truth of these sources, and, more importantly, perceives the person of Christ manifested through these sources, by the virtue of *faith*. While philosophical and theological argument can help show the coherence or reasonableness of Catholic conceptions of God, and while aspects of the Catholic conception of God can be rationally demonstrated, the person of Christ and the truth of the *entire* Catholic conception of God can only be perceived and believed in, not demonstrated. Faith is an intellectual habit given by God, which enables a person to believe these sources, grasp their reasonableness, and holistically perceive the person of Christ as revealed through them (*ST* II–II q.1–4; Balthasar 2009). Because of this reliance on faith, this Element can at most help to show the coherence of those conceptions, explain their historical and philosophical bases, and, most importantly, provide a witness to what I, as a Catholic, have perceived by faith. Since Catholicism conceives of its conception of God as ordered to facilitating personal relations with God, that conception cannot be fully presented apart from giving such a witness.

God is conceived here as one who reveals himself, primarily in the holistic way in which persons relate to other persons, but also in a propositionally expressible way (Stump 2010: 39–63). God is intelligible, one who can be understood. God has authority to guide and teach others, and this authority is expressed through a concrete community, the Church. God created finite persons so that they could be parts of this Church, the community of those who have grace or are being deified. Deification means coming to share in God's life, taking on his charity or self-giving love, so that one loves, acts, and understands as God does, and so that one is a child of God, loved by God as he loves himself, thereby sharing in being God (Spezzano 2015; Meconi 2018). In each of these ways, God is *participated* or *shared in* by creatures: God shares what belongs essentially to him (like intelligibility or authority) with creatures, such that those properties exist partially in creatures and those creatures are dependent on and receptive to God (Aquinas 1954a).

The bishops at the First Council of Nicaea (325) formulated a Creed, or statement of belief, to express what they took to be the core of the tradition's conception of God; this Creed was further developed at the First Council of Constantinople (381) (D 150). It is said during many Catholic liturgies. According to this Creed, God is Trinitarian, that is, there is one God, and that God is three persons: Father, Son, and Holy Spirit. On this conception, God has the properties ascribed to him on the view often called "classical theism" (Davies 2004: 2–9). For example, God is simple, not composed of parts; he entirely transcends creatures, being more dissimilar than similar to them (D 800, 806, 3001); he is eternal, having complete, simultaneous possession of life, rather than having life distended into multiple, changing moments; and he is omnipresent, present at all places, in that he is aware of them and has causal power over them (*ST* I q.10, a.1–2). God has all perfections – properties that do not intrinsically involve some lack and that are better to have than not have (Garrigou-Lagrange 1938: 131–3). Since he already has all perfections, he is impassible, unable to be affected such that he could gain a perfection from another (Pawl 2016: 16–18).

The three divine persons are one in being or "consubstantial" (*homoousios*) (D 125). Each person equally and identically has the attributes mentioned earlier (Emery 2010). Generally, Catholic theologians have understood the persons to be distinct due to their relations to one another. (More will be said on this in Section 2.) The Father has no source but is the one who begets the Son. The Son is the person begotten by the Father; he is the Word who perfectly expresses all that the Father is. With the question of how the Holy Spirit relates to the Father and the Son, we come to a first tension within the Catholic conception of God. Western Catholics (those whose traditions originate in western Europe and western North Africa) understand the Spirit to proceed from the Father and the Son, as the expression of their love for one another. This formulation was one point of division between Western Catholics and the Eastern Orthodox, whose churches divided during the Middle Ages. On the Orthodox view, the Spirit proceeds from the Father, not the Son; Eastern theologians emphasize that the Father is the ultimate principle of all things, created and divine, and worry that seeing Father and Son as co-sources of the Spirit obscures that claim. (Other worries will be considered in Section 2.) Some bridge this divide by holding that the Spirit proceeds from the Father *through* the Son: the Father is the source of all divine power and love, but he shares this power with the Son. This formulation was adopted by Eastern Catholics, whose traditions originate in Eastern Europe, the Middle East, Egypt, Ethiopia, and India; most Eastern Catholic traditions originate in groups of Orthodox Christians who came back into union with the Catholic Church at various points since the sixteenth century. This formulation is also endorsed by Western theologians like St. Thomas Aquinas (1225–74) and St. Bonaventure (1221–74) (*ST* I, q.36, a.3; Bonaventure 1882: 220–1; Pontifical Council for Promoting Christian Unity 1995). This debate shows that, even at the level of its fundamental conception of God, Catholicism allows for variation and debate.

Catholics believe that the Son became incarnate (that is, became human) in Jesus Christ. The Son joined a created human nature to himself, without ceasing to be divine (*ST* III q.1–3), to save human persons from sin and to deify us. To sin is to alienate oneself from God by willingly pursuing some ultimate end other than God. Catholics hold that God is our ultimate end, the one who alone can perfectly fulfill us, and to whom (as perfect goodness and our first cause) we owe love, obedience, and praise. Once we have sinful tendencies (and, in what is called "original sin," all human persons after the first sin have such tendencies and alienation from God, unless they receive special divine assistance), we cannot by our own effort direct ourselves to our proper end and love God as we ought. But since he is divine, Christ *does* live out infinitely perfect love, and, since he is human, he does this through our nature. In this way, a human being – a being who has our nature and acts through its powers and is one who owes God love, obedience, and praise – offers God even more than what we owe him. In this way, Christ overcomes sin, and his human nature is deified. Because we, like Christ, have human nature and because we can be joined to Christ through his body, the Church, we too can receive deification. Christ's acts "atone" for our sins, that is, they make us and our nature "at one" or unified with God (Scheeben 1946: 405–68; Balthasar 1994b; Anselm 1998: 260–356).

In the Incarnation and atonement, we see the divine attributes of mercy and love (or charity), which are central to any Catholic conception of God. God is omnipotent, able to do anything not self-contradictory, but this omnipotence (along with divine goodness) is especially revealed in acts of "sparing and having mercy" (Roman Missal, Collect for the Tenth Sunday after Pentecost). Mercy is God's orientation to give others more than their just due; it manifests the love or charity that he fundamentally is – the free and constant orientation to give goods to others. God's love and mercy motivate all his acts, from acts of self-gift among the divine persons to creation, Incarnation, and deification. As with all divine attributes, these are oriented to being shared with others. In the practice of "works of mercy," like feeding the hungry or instructing the ignorant, Catholics understand themselves to act in a way motivated by God's own self-giving love, in which they share. Just as the Son humbly took on a lower nature and expressed love through service and suffering, so we are empowered to act mercifully and humbly for others. These dispositions are expressed in Catholic spiritualities, such as the "little way" of St. Thérèse of Lisieux (1873–97), in which one does every act and undergoes every suffering, no matter how small, motivated by God's self-emptying love (Thérèse 2006). These dispositions are also found in Catholic devotions, like those to the Sacred Heart of Jesus or to Divine Mercy. Both these devotions arose through revelations in which Jesus is believed by many Catholics to have appeared to St. Margaret Mary Alacoque (1647–90) and St. Faustina Kowalska (1905–38), respectively. Catholic conceptions of God are often colored not only by the "public" revelation of Scripture and Tradition but also by "private" revelations, special experiences of God by particular persons, the content of which is approved and passed on by the Church.

This emphasis on divine charity and goodness raises some problems regarding God. If God is perfectly good, then he must be just, giving everyone their due. Catholic liturgies present God as "judge of the living and the dead" (Roman Missal, Nicene Creed) and as "just judge of vengeance" (Roman Missal, Dies Irae). God punishes and rewards both in our current life and after death. But if God is just, it would seem he cannot be merciful since mercy seems to violate justice, by failing to give to others what is owed to them (Anselm 1998: 91–4). Yet, God is also understood to be always ready to forgive and heal, as in the Sacraments of Confession and Anointing of the Sick, even though forgiveness and healing are not deserved in justice. At times, some Catholics' practices and preaching have emphasized God's justice, so that God was conceived as distant and wrathful; at other times, God has been conceived of as merciful to the point that the seriousness of sin, as opposed to goodness itself, has almost been denied (Turek 2022: 13–19). This is one case of a broader philosophical problem: many attributes ascribed to God, like mercy and justice, or transcendence and immanence, seem to be logically, metaphysically, or morally incompatible. A second problem is that if God is impassible, then it does not seem that God can be just *or* merciful. These are reactive or responsive attitudes, but something impassible, it would seem, cannot respond to anything since responsiveness seems to require that one first *receive* knowledge of that to which one responds (Stump 2003: 115–22). I return to this second problem in Section 3.

To solve these problems, Catholicism does not reject one of any pair of properties that we have reason to ascribe to God but conceives of God as a "coincidence of opposites." Each of any such pair is understood to be a distinct manifestation of the perfect goodness that God is; the paired properties are not understood to be contradictories (Cousins 1978). For example, a good being must manifest both justice and mercy, and mercy is not opposed to justice but, rather, is a way of meeting the demands of justice. Problems like this have fruitfully developed the Catholic conception of God: if each of two apparently opposed claims about God are well supported, then Catholics tend to be willing to affirm both, even before grasping *how* both can be true, in trust, both in God's revelation and in the power of human reason, that a solution will be found (Chesterton 2001: 117–50).

A key pair of divine attributes in the Catholic conception of God is *transcendence and immanence*. Grasping the importance of this pair requires understanding a distinctive kind of reasoning in Catholic thought. While Catholicism reasons about God using standard logical inferences, it also engages in *reasoning by fittingness*, in which one considers which claims *fit* with (or can be harmonized with) some given claim. This is an *aesthetic* style of reasoning: one must *perceive* how claims illumine one another or render one another more intelligible, and thereby perceive how they contribute to a beautiful, perceivable whole (Narcisse 1997). Catholicism has defined dogmas on this basis. The dogma that Mary, the mother of Jesus, was conceived without original sin, was defined, in part, on the grounds that it was fitting for Jesus to be conceived by a sinless mother: it shows well the extent of Jesus' salvific acts (in that they extend even to a person who was conceived before those acts), it honors Jesus' divinity, and it honors Mary, who consented to share in God's salvific plan (D 2801). Catholicism has also defended doctrines with these arguments, such as by arguing that the Incarnation, while not strictly necessary, was a most fitting way for God to save us from sin (*ST* III q.1, a.1). Catholic theologians have also thought about transcendence and immanence using such reasoning. While God transcends the created world, God the Son has entered creation by joining a created nature to himself. It does not *strictly* follow from this that God is present in *all* creatures, but it *fits* well with the pattern set by the Incarnation that God is immanent, acting through the mediation of all created, physical things (Feingold 2021), though the Incarnation is an entirely unique mode of divine presence. This conception of divine immanence is sometimes called an *incarnational* or *sacramental* conception of God, a sacrament being a created thing by which God makes himself present to us.

This conception of God's relation to the world fits with the view that creatures, including bodies, are real and of value in themselves, and not just expressions of God's will. Early on, the Church rejected Docetism, according to which the Son only appeared to take on human nature and suffering, but did not really do so. Rather, on the Catholic view, human nature and suffering really exist and the Son really assumed them (D 301). But given that Christ is the definitive revelation of God, it *fits* with Docetism to hold that human nature, suffering, and other creatures do not exist or have value properly speaking, but only God does (Loudovikos 2019: 1–11). That view in turn fits with, and renders more intelligible, some versions of the problem of evil, on which it is claimed that if God existed, there could not be evil, including suffering. Such a God, for whom all things are merely a manifestation of his will, would want to stop evil and would be able to stop it. So, either evil or God do not exist.

Given its incarnational views, Catholicism does not conceive of God's relation to the world in this way. Rather, a distinctive solution to the problem of evil fits with Catholicism's conception of God. We can see this solution by considering the related problem of why a perfect God would create at all. On the Catholic conception, God does not have needs or lacks that could be fulfilled by creation, nor does he create necessarily (D 3025). Rather, he creates freely out of love, to give himself to others and to allow others to give themselves to each other and to him. What he loves is this real, historical world; it is through *this* world, with its actual history, including its evil, that we know God. In the Incarnation, God reveals himself to be oriented to defeating evil by entering history and suffering evil out of love and solidarity with us. Christ's death on the Cross reveals that evil, suffering, and death are not (as in Docetism) illusions, nor is suffering something a loving God could just have willed not to exist. Rather, since human freedom is real, not merely an expression of God's will, evil results from misused freedom. It can only be defeated by enabling human freedom to be used well, which Christ did through the Cross. Furthermore, unlike in those religions in which suffering is entirely something to be overcome, on the Catholic conception, lovingly enduring suffering has, through the Cross, become a means to union with God. Sharing in suffering can be a way of sharing in the divine life of self-giving love and a means of offering one's life to God; by our suffering, we can share in the Son's perfect self-offering to the Father (Balthasar 1994b, 1998; Stump 2010).

God, on the Catholic conception, gives growth in virtue and deification not just through suffering but, more importantly, through the seven Sacraments. While all things are sacraments in the sense that all things manifest God, the seven Sacraments are ecclesially sanctioned material things, actions, and words by which God brings about deification in human persons whenever those things are used, actions are performed, and words said with a correct intention by an appropriate minister; they are signs that make present what they signify (Feingold 2021: 62–3, 466–75). For example, Catholics believe that God comes to dwell in human persons through baptism: when water is poured on a person and the right words said, God lives and acts in that person. God has created creatures to reveal himself and provide means to union with him (*ST* III, q.74). Acts that reveal God also include the recitation or chanting of Psalms and prayers eight times a day, which is known as the Divine Office, and, most importantly for Catholics, the Mass or Divine Liturgy, the ritual that centers around the Eucharist, the Sacrament in which bread and wine become the body and blood of Jesus, and Jesus' sacrifice on the Cross is made present to us. In the Eucharist, we *perceive* all aspects of the Catholic conception of God: The incarnate Son, out of loving mercy, becomes available to us as food so that we can be entirely united to him and thereby become deified; hence, the Eucharist is called the "source and summit" of the faith (D 4127).

1.2 The Jewish and Greek Inheritance of Catholicism

From the Jewish tradition, the Catholic Church drew the conception of God as creator, as involved in history, and as revealed through bodily things. God is above all revealed through covenants he makes with particular people, especially the people of Israel, which Catholics see as preparing for the Incarnation. Rather than just being discovered by our efforts, God takes the initiative in relating to us: he elects certain persons and groups, not because of their merits but to reveal his righteousness and fidelity. He promises to deliver them from concrete evils, commands them to follow moral and religious laws, aids them in following those laws, and punishes or rewards them. God has sovereign, but not capricious, freedom. As creator and deliverer, God is worthy of being worshiped through interior sacrifice of our lives and exterior sacrifices like loving acts and blood sacrifices. The world is meant to be physically dedicated back to God, and both kinds of sacrifice make us "at one" with God by returning to him creatures that reveal him. God's attributes are here conceived primarily in moral terms: he is merciful, righteous, faithful, peaceful, and yet jealous for our worship. God is conceived in contrast to idols, anything other than God to which we might dedicate our lives. But he is also conceived in erotic terms, as one who elects Israel to be his bride and who loves her passionately, in a way imaged in marital love. Finally, not only is God revealed through history, but history is conceived eschatologically: God moves history toward a final fulfillment, when he will definitively reveal himself through a savior, a Messiah (Keefe 1991; Balthasar 1991b; Schoeman 2003; Spencer 2022a).

From the Jewish tradition, Catholicism draws a conception of God as one who takes the initiative in his relationship to us and who elects and sends persons (especially Jesus) on missions (Garrigou-Lagrange 1946b; Balthasar 1992: 149–282). As it was in the priesthood and kingship of Israel, so now God's authority is incarnated in the institution of the Catholic Church, despite the sinfulness of its members. As he did for Israel, so now God gives this Church specific, sacrificial ways of worshipping him and definite laws to follow. Especially in the mystical tradition (considered in Section 4), God is conceived of as our lover. The prohibition on idols and the conception of God as righteous, faithful, and jealous for our worship are also retained, as is the eschatological view of time. However, on the Catholic view, God has, in Christ, already brought about final fulfillment, though this fulfillment has not been as fully revealed as it will be at the end of history.

Catholicism has also, from its earliest days, drawn upon the Greek philosophical tradition (Balthasar 1989; Bradshaw 2007; Perl 2014). The Greek conception of God is partly consonant with the Jewish conception and partly in tension with it. The New Testament (and parts of the Old) was influenced by Stoicism and Platonism, and these influences on the Church grew over subsequent centuries. On these traditions, abstracting from their differences, God is a universal agent, the source of all things; he is naturally knowable by any rational being, reasoning from created effects to their first cause. These classical theist views are consistent with most Jewish conceptions. God is the unity of the whole cosmos, or the transcendent One and Good, in which all things participate for their unity and goodness. On some Platonist views, God either is or directly gives rise to a Word or Mind (*Logos* or *Nous*), in which are contained the ideas (*logoi*) of all things, and a Spirit or Soul (*Pneuma* or *Psuche*), which gives life to all living things. God has providence, intelligent care, over all things. Unlike on the Jewish view, God does not elect particular nations to have a distinct relationship with him, and history is conceived cyclically: the world manifests God through history's cycles. God is not passionately in love with us but is the highest object of our *eros* or desire. Bodily goods and desires only imitate and approach God remotely and can distract us from God. Moral virtue, liturgical ritual, and intellectual contemplation, by contrast, bring us closer to God. God can only be grasped intellectually or by transcending intellectual activity; this view led many Catholics to an ascetic spirituality and an emphasis on intellectual (rather than sensory) experience in approaching God.

But Catholicism also drew on Greek polytheism, in which the divine is multiple and (as on the Jewish view) calls for sacrifice and devotion, and approaches us erotically. Catholics tend to synthesize practices, experiences, and conceptions of God from many religious traditions. Catholicism is monotheistic and opposed to idolatry but still conceives of God as multiple persons, as including personal differences and dependencies. The Catholic tradition has applied to the Trinitarian person imagery drawn from the Greek gods (Balthasar 1989: 43–154; Rahner 2021). On some Greek views, the first cause of all things, the One, necessarily gives rise to other "ones," that is, other gods. While Catholicism denies that divine persons are distinct gods, it drew on this view in formulating the doctrine of the Father as the principle of the Son and the Spirit (Hankey 2019). As Joseph Ratzinger (Pope Benedict XVI [1927–2022]) says, following St. Maximus the Confessor (580–662), Catholicism reconciled Greek polytheism and Jewish monotheism (Ratzinger 2004: 125). Furthermore, the polytheist tendency to see aspects of human life as standing under the patronage of gods has a place in Catholic conceptions of the divine, in the cult of saints and angels (non-bodily, intelligent beings). Saints and angels are gods not by nature but in the sense that they are deified persons who share in and make present to us the life of God, mediating God's providence to us and our prayers to God (Wiitala 2019). Again, Catholicism conceives of divinity as sharable. However, while finding these truths in polytheism, Catholicism also distances itself from that tradition by holding that the three divine persons share one, numerically same, nature and that they are distinct persons in a sense of "person" only analogous to personhood as found among nondivine beings. These ideas will be explained further in the following.

1.3 Philosophical Problems from Greek and Jewish Inheritances

Although ancient Jewish and Greek traditions influenced one another, Catholics have often experienced this dual inheritance as leading to tensions. These are expressed by the Church Father, Tertullian (155–220), who asked what Athens

(Greek tradition) has to do with Jerusalem (Jewish tradition). Blaise Pascal (1623–62) contrasts the living "God of Abraham, Isaac, and Jacob" to the abstract "God of the [Greek] philosophers," which he dismisses as unable to vitally affect us (Pascal 2008: 178). Many theologians have since argued that Catholic conceptions of God should be purged of Hellenistic elements in order to focus on the more Jewish, existentially relevant roots of that conception (Benedict XVI 2006). Some Greek philosophical views Docetistically denigrate the physical world, including the human body, which God assumed and redeemed in the Incarnation. They lack the dramatic, eschatologically oriented interplay between God and creatures found in the Jewish view, on which God has concretely delivered us from evils. The trust in God that the Greek philosophical view engenders is trust in the conclusion of a sound argument, not trust in a loving person. Greek reasoning can lead to the hubristic view that our concepts fully capture all that God is, as the fourth century Eunomius of Cyzicus thought. This is contrary both to the humility displayed on the Cross and necessary for deification and to the transcendence of God over all that can be thought of him. Because of its hubris, the Greek view gave rise to heresies (officially rejected conceptions of God) like *Pelagianism*, on which we naturally have all that we need to move toward union with God, rather than needing to receive God's free, personal gifts (Brown 2000: 340–99). Only a God who passionately loves us, with whom we can enter a relationship and who is moved by love to enter history and save us, is worthy of worship. This conception is found more in the Jewish tradition than in the Greek.

But others in Catholic history, like Marcion (85–160), rejected the Jewish conception of God as morally offensive. A God who is jealous, who commands violence (say, in blood sacrifice), and who apparently arbitrarily elects only some persons for relationship with himself cannot be the God revealed in Christ's merciful love, who matches the Greek conception of God as pure goodness (Hart 2003: 349). The Greek tradition conceives of God in universal terms, as beauty, goodness, being, consciousness, or happiness in themselves. We experience the divine by reasoning from particular beings and their partial perfections to the universal, absolute perfections in which they participate. God should not be conceived of as "a" being, but as being itself, in which all other beings share (Hart 2013). For God to be worthy of our worship, he must be not only perfect, eternal, and not moved by creaturely evil but also sovereignly transcendent, able to make us, like him, unaffected by evil. Marcion and others see the Jewish conception as depicting a morally ambivalent, mutable, and passable God, who is not, to them, worthy of our worship. But given the Greek conception, it is easy for them to see why God alone is worthy of our worship: God is beauty, goodness, truth, unity, and being themselves; all other beings exist only through participation in him, as his manifestations or icons, and so all other beings direct any attention or worship we would pay them to him.

The Catholic tradition does not leave any genuine experience of the divine out of its conception of God but incorporates them all regardless of what tensions this might produce. Catholicism takes an analogical or symphonic approach (explained further in Section 4) to this synthesis, in which we recognize the similarities and differences between the Jewish and Greek approaches and adopt them both, seeing each as a distinct viewpoint upon the truth (Tracy 1981; Balthasar 1987). It has disposed Catholicism to incorporate other cultures' conceptions of God (or of what is of absolute importance) into itself, though this opens Catholicism to deviations in various directions. Catholicism sees analogies between revelations of God in other cultures and the supreme revelation of God in Christ. Some theologians and local Catholic traditions have incorporated into their conception of God, for example, the Germanic focus on God's concern for honor, the Zen Buddhist emphasis on apophatic meditation as a route to the absolute, and the Lakota awareness of God's activity in the natural world (Johnston 1970; Anselm 1998: 260–356; Costello 2005).

2 Trinitarian and Incarnational Controversies

In this section, I turn to the next stage of the history of the Catholic conception of God, the formulating of the doctrines of the Trinity and the Incarnation in the early councils, and the development of these doctrines in the Middle Ages. I consider problems that these doctrines occasioned; I also consider how they solved aspects of problems like the tension between Greek and Jewish experiences of God. Throughout, I emphasize terms that the Church uses to express these doctrines, like "person" and "nature." The development of doctrine in Catholicism is generally understood as a process of making explicit what was previously only implicitly grasped or a logically coherent growth of an earlier idea in light of new problems and external circumstances (Newman 1994; Garrigou-Lagrange 2021: pt. 3).

2.1 The Trinity

The early Catholic Church faced the problem of grasping how Christ's actions, especially his sacrifice on the Cross, reveal God and reconcile us to him, allowing us to overcome our sinful habits and to be deified or achieve union with God. In solving this problem, the Fathers adhered to general logical and philosophical principles, such as: if two things are each identical to a third, then those two things are identical to each other, and if one thing has some property, but another thing lacks that property, then those two things are distinct (for background on this section's themes, see: Ayers 2006; Radde-Gallwitz 2009; Emery 2010; White 2015; Pawl 2020; Pfau 2022: 127–219; White 2022).

The New Testament and Christian tradition present God as Father, Son, and Holy Spirit (e.g., *Matthew* 28:19) and as one (e.g., *Mark* 12:29). But if God is one, and the Father, the Son, and the Holy Spirit are identical to God, then it would seem to follow that they are identical to one another. With *modalism* or *Sabellianism* (after the third century Sabellius), we might conclude, using the logical principles mentioned at the end of the previous paragraph, that the "Father," the "Son," and the "Holy Spirit" are just names of that one God or of ways that God manifests himself or that they are three of his roles. But Scripture represents the Father, the Son, and the Holy Spirit doing distinct things; for example, the Son, but not the Father or the Holy Spirit, became human, died, and rose. If each of these is God, then we might conclude, with *tritheism*, that there are three Gods, perhaps with one universal divine nature instantiated in three particulars. But this is inconsistent with the conclusion of classical philosophy that there is only one first cause or God and with Scripture's testimony to monotheism. Given that the Father, the Son, and the Holy Spirit are distinct, that there is just one God, that God is simple, and that Scripture says that the Son and the Spirit are dependent upon the Father, it seems to follow (as *subordinationism*, *Arianism* [after Arius (256–336)], and *Eunomianism* [after Eunomius of Cyzicus] held) that the Father alone is the one first, simple, uncaused cause. The Son and the Spirit would then be creatures, made by the Father and subordinate to him, though participating preeminently in his divine nature.

Each of these views avoids the logical difficulties that seem to follow from saying that the Father, the Son, and the Spirit are both identical to the one God and distinct from one another; yet, each of them is inconsistent with desiderata for a Christian conception of God (D 112–15). Creatures are finite, limited, and dependent beings, while God is infinite, unlimited, and not dependent; God has perfections essentially and intrinsically, while creatures have properties through participation. Creatures are radically distinct in kind and ontological status from God; to share in a creature's properties would be to share in God in a mediated, partial, and imperfect way, not to share in God's very nature. Everything that participates in some perfection only imperfectly reveals and is one with that perfection. But it is central to the Catholic conception of God that Christ perfectly reveals God and makes us able to share in God's nature. If the Son were merely a creature, then Christ would not perfectly reveal God but would only reveal God imperfectly; in being joined to him, we would be joined to a mere creature, not to God, and so he could not make us one with God.

Likewise, the Spirit is understood to deify us, uniting us to the Father and the Son. For the same reasons that apply to the Son, the Spirit could not do this if he were not God. Views like those of the *Pneumatomachians* or *Macedonians*, who denied that the Spirit is God, must also be rejected on the Catholic conception.

The Catholic solutions to these problems were worked out at the First Council of Nicaea (D 125–26) and the First Council of Constantinople (D 150–77). The decisions reached at these councils drew on and were elucidated by Fathers like St. Athanasius (296–373), St. Gregory Nazianzus (325–89), St. Basil the Great (329–79), and St. Gregory of Nyssa (335–95) (Gregory of Nyssa 1893; Basil 1980; Athanasius 1996; Gregory of Nazianzus 2002). They introduced the key terms used in the conception of God shared by Catholics and many Orthodox and Protestants. While different thinkers use these terms in different, conflicting ways, my focus here is on how they were systematically used in the Catholic solution to problems about God.

First, God is one *nature* or *substance* (Greek *ousia*; Latin *essentia* or *substantia*). Second, God is three persons (Greek *hypostaseis* or *prosopa*; Latin *supposita* or *personae*) (for more details on these terms, see Hipp 2012). A *nature* is "what" something is; it is that concrete principle in a thing which corresponds to a definition or description of its kind and which is the source of its acting in ways typical of its kind. A *person* is a "who," someone who has or possesses a nature and who performs activities in virtue of it. Medieval Catholic scholastics understood persons to be *incommunicable*, unable to belong to another as, for example, a part belongs to a whole or as a universal belongs to a particular; rather, a person possesses itself, its nature, and its acts. While all concrete particulars of any kind are incommunicable (each one is a *hypostasis* [Greek] or a *suppositum* [Latin]), a *person* is both incommunicable and intellectual or spiritual, having powers to grasp any being and to freely will and love any good (Richard of St. Victor 1855: 945–7; Aquinas 1856: bk.3, d.5, q.2, a.1, ad2). Some Catholic personalists have argued that, since persons possess their spiritual acts, to be an incommunicable person is to have these acts under one's governance, to experience them subjectively, and, by these acts, to be able to make a gift of oneself to another. To be a person is, in part, to stand in relation to others (Clarke 1993; Crosby 1996: 41–81).

According to the teaching of the early councils, the Father, the Son, and the Spirit are each equally God; they are *consubstantial* or *homoousios* with each other – that is, these persons have just one nature, one divinity, and one source of divine action. The Father, the Son, and the Spirit are not instances of a universal divine nature, nor are they three parts of a divine whole. Rather, they are each an incommunicable possessor of numerically one divine nature, of the acts performed through that nature, and of the attributes that belong to it. The Catholic understanding of these doctrines was developed at medieval councils like the Fourth Lateran Council (1215) and the Council of Florence (1439–45), where it was held that what distinguishes divine persons is their relations to and processions from one another (D 800, 803–06, 1330–31). The Father is God without principle but begets the Son; the Son is God begotten by the Father; the Spirit is God poured out by the Father through or with the Son.

This relational account of persons answers the logical problem of how these three persons can be one in nature, while being distinct from each other. Since God is pure, simple perfection and actuality, he cannot take on additional perfection or actuality; it is impossible to add perfection to one who already has all perfections. The persons cannot add to the divine nature any perfection, and yet they must add *something* to that nature. Scholastic solutions to this problem include two points. First, relations add to substances or natures in a distinctive way: a relation is a way that a substance is referred to something. One substance can, in itself, be referred to multiple *relata*, without those relations being the same as one another. These relations do not add any perfection to the substance but belong to the substance in itself. For example, the road between Athens and Thebes is one with the uphill relation from one city to another and one with the opposite downhill relation from the second city back to the first, but these relations are distinct from one another. So, likewise, the relations constitutive of the divine persons are one with the divine nature but not the same as one another. Second, to say that the persons are identical in the sense of being consubstantial is not to say that they are identical in the strict sense to which logical laws like the law of transitivity of identity apply. Rather, there is a distinction between the personal relations and the nature, such that what belongs to one person need not belong to another (*ST* I q.28; Aquinas 1954b: bk.3, lect.5; Emery 2010: 84–95, 115–41). The problem of what kind of distinction obtains between the relations and the nature will be considered in Section 3.

According to Catholic doctrine, neither divine nature nor divine personhood is privileged over the other. Some Eastern theologians have worried that, on the Western Catholic view, according to which the Holy Spirit proceeds from the Father *and* the Son, God's nature is unduly privileged over the divine persons. If the Father and the Son act as a joint principle of the Spirit, then (on the Platonist metaphysics held by many Christian theologians) they must act in virtue of some shared principle of unity, and this would be the shared nature. Some Eastern theologians worry that this fits best with a view on which the divine nature is a thing distinct from the persons, in which they participate, and so which is superior or prior to them. The real first principle of all things, then, would be a nonpersonal nature, not the divine persons. This argument from fittingness, which if successful would show the Western Catholic view to be incompatible with a conception of God as fully personal, is blocked by the teaching that the divine nature wholly belongs to each person and is not a "fourth thing" distinct from the persons (D 800–06). Likewise, the divine persons are not privileged over the nature: it is not the case that a divine person could, say, freely decide on the content of the nature, nor is one of the persons (say, the Father) a principle or cause of the nature (Balthasar 2004: 135–49). Rather, as we saw in Section 1, God is a "coincidence of opposites." God equally fundamentally includes natural perfection and personal incommunicability. Both concrete terms like "a being," "a good person," and "an agent" and abstract terms like "being itself," "goodness itself," and "causality itself" apply to God (*ST* I, q.3, a.3).

2.2 God Incarnate

The next five ecumenical councils considered how to conceive of God incarnate. We saw in Section 1 that, to accomplish the purpose of the incarnation, Christ must be human. This is so that our human nature can be united to God and so that Christ's self-sacrifice is offered by a human being, that is, by one who owes God such an offering. We must be able to share in Christ's body, that is, be parts of his Church. This occurs through Sacraments like Baptism, Confirmation, and Eucharist. But to become parts of Christ's body, we must already have a nature that he has. We also saw in Section 1 that, to accomplish the purpose of the Incarnation, Christ must be divine, so that we are united to God when we are united to Christ and so that his self-offering will be of infinite value (Athanasius 1996: 31–47; Anselm 1998: 260–356; *ST* III, q.49). A problem for the Catholic conception of God regards *how* Christ can be both human and God. The language of *nature* and *person* can solve this problem too, but it contributes to further problems.

Given that an account of the Incarnation is meant to explain how human beings can be forgiven and deified, it might initially make sense to think that Jesus is God in the same sense that we are meant to become God. Just as we come to share in God's nature, acts, life, and love, so the first-century Jewish man Jesus of Nazareth came to participate in them but in a preeminent way. Since he allowed God to act through him, God was manifested in him. God's self-sacrificing love is especially seen in how he died for others on the Cross. On this *adoptionist* view, this man was rewarded by maximal participation in God after his resurrection; Jesus was thereby "adopted" as God's son and is the pattern for our own adoption and deification. The language of "nature" and *hypostasis* allows us to formulate a similar view. Among mere creatures, each nature is possessed by one *hypostasis*, and each *hypostasis* has just one nature: there is just one answer to the question of "what" each thing substantially is. We might then affirm, with *Nestorianism* (after Nestorius [386–450]), that Jesus is both divine and human and, yet, hold that this means that he is two *hypostaseis* or persons, each with a distinct nature (D 251a–251e; Balthasar 2005: 37–9). To say that Jesus is a single person with both a divine and human nature would, it seems to entail some contradictions. If Jesus is divine, then he is without an origin in time, impassible, simple, cannot suffer or die, and so forth. If Jesus is human, then he has an origin in time, is passible, composite, suffered and died, and so forth (Pawl 2016). But, on this Nestorian view, we can say that the divine and human *hypostaseis* in Jesus are one "person" in the looser sense (Greek *prosopon*) that they appear, act, and will totally as one, with a single "face" (Pfau 2022: 164–78).

Neither of these views makes sense of Scriptural and liturgical claims about the divinity of Jesus, and neither gives an adequate basis for atonement. If Jesus is just a man joined to God by adoption or unity of will and action, that does not explain how *he* is reconciled or united to God. If God is willing to deify a human person by sheer will in Jesus' case, then there is no reason for Jesus to suffer and die to make us one with God; God could deify us in the same way. To be the cause of our deification, one person must be both divine and human.

Scripture and tradition witness to Jesus' sinlessness; his whole life was one of constant obedience and loving self-offering to the Father. But human nature seems to be oriented to sin, and we sin with our minds and wills. Hence, *Appollinarianism* (after the fourth century Apollinaris of Laodicea) held that the sinless Son could only join to himself the parts of human nature that are not the causes of sin; he took on a human body and a human soul insofar as it is the principle that makes the body alive but not a human mind or will. On this view, Jesus is the Son of God, with divine nature, mind, and will, joined to human soul and flesh. But were this the case, then the whole of human nature would not have been redeemed: the powers with which we sin, mind and will, would not be "at one" with God (D 146). The Fathers frequently affirm that whatever is not joined to the Son is not redeemed (Balthasar 1992: 237–45). The Son must have taken on all human nature but without a disposition to sin. This shows that, on the Catholic view, human nature in itself is not oriented to sin. Rather, sin is a misuse of good human nature, which is ordered to union with God especially through mind and will (*ST* I–II q.85).

Yet, as we have seen, it seems that each *hypostasis* has one nature and vice versa. We might then affirm with *monophysitism* that, in becoming incarnate, the human and divine natures joined, such that Jesus has one "theandric" (from *theos*, God and *anthropos*, human) nature and principle of action. Such a view preserves divine immanence: In becoming human, God the Son became truly "God with us"; he truly lowered himself, taking on our human condition, in such a way that what he is, is a joining of the divine and human. However, this view does not preserve God's transcendence over creatures. God is simple, immutable, impassible, and already contains all perfection. The divine nature cannot change such that it would enter composition with another nature.

The Catholic conception of God incarnate that solved these problems was worked out at the Council of Ephesus in 431, the Council of Chalcedon in 451, and the Second Council of Constantinople in 553 (D 250–66, 300–03, 422–38). On this conception, Jesus is one person (*prosopon, persona, hypostasis,* and *suppositum*) in two natures (*ousiai* and *essentiae*), which are joined in that person "without confusion, without change, without division, [and] without separation" (D 302). Each nature retains all its attributes, powers, and acts, but all those belong inseparably to the one person. Jesus is both passible and impassible, in the sense that he has a nature that is passible and a nature that is impassible; those properties are not opposed (Pawl 2016). The divine nature remains transcendent, impassible, and simple, not entering into composition with human nature. The human nature is created, passible, and composite. The person, not the nature, joins the natures, and, as we have seen, a person is just that which possesses natures. Yet, it is the one divine person, the Son, who performs all of his human and divine acts; in this way, human nature is entirely and perfectly joined to God, our redemption and deification are made possible, and God is perfectly revealed through Jesus' human actions.

While it is not part of the official teaching of the Church, recent Catholic personalist philosophy deepens a Catholic conception of God by showing *how* and *why* multiple natures can be joined in divine *persons* (Crosby 1996: 161–73). We grasp in reflection upon our own personhood that to be a person is to be *open to the world*. We are not restricted to grasping and seeking just what biologically stimulates us, but can grasp and will any nature, as such. We persons are open to receiving any nature, according to the capacity of the powers that belong to our natures. It is only in our limited human power to take on new natures by receiving them into our minds, not receiving them substantially. But a person of unlimited power could not just receive other natures in his mind but could substantially take on natures because of the world-openness that belongs to persons as such This happened in the *hypostatic union* of the two natures in the one person of Christ.

The councils safeguard the claim that everything in both natures fully belongs to the person of the Son by affirming that Mary, Jesus' mother, is the "God-bearer" (*Theotokos*) and the "Mother of God" (D 272, 300). What Mary, like any mother, bore is not just a human nature but a *person* – in this case, a divine person, the Son. This sets up a pattern of reasoning for Catholic conceptions of God: claims about God (and about our own potential for deification) are safeguarded by claims about Mary, with whom God has a distinct kind of union, since Mary bore a divine person. For example, that Jesus rose from the dead and that human bodies can be deified are upheld by affirming that Mary's body was taken into heaven at the end of her earthly life (Sheen 1952: 112–22; de Koninck 2009).

This Catholic conception of God incarnate was furthered by the sixth and seventh ecumenical councils. Even among those who agreed that Christ had a complete human nature, distinct from his divine nature, the problem of Christ's sinlessness remained (Pawl 2019: 132–66). It is difficult to make sense of the idea that Christ had a human will, a power for intellectually loving and desiring goods, intending ends, and choosing means, distinct from his divine will. It seems reasonable to think, with *monothelitism*, that it is *persons*, not natures, that have wills since it is persons that love, choose, and so forth, and that since Christ always willed sinlessly and was a divine person, he only had a divine will (Greek *thelema*, Latin *voluntas*). Yet, as St. Maximus the Confessor saw, this is no better than monophysitism. If the Son did not assume *all* of human nature and *all* human powers, including the human power to will – that is, to will in a finite way, on the basis of human understanding – then not all of human nature is redeemed and deified. We sin and are estranged from God primarily through our willing. The purpose of the Son becoming human was so that he could offer perfect, infinite love and obedience to the Father *as a human being* and so that we, who have the same nature, could thereby be joined to that perfect offering, and all the damage to our nature from sin could be healed. One can only love and obey *as a human* with *human* power and the act of willing. So, the Son must have taken on a human will, as affirmed at the Third Council of Constantinople (680–81). But this does not mean that Christ, by his human will, ever willed sinfully, contrary to the divine will. Rather, he humanly willed only in obedience to, and at the prompting of, his divine willing (D 553–8; Maximus 2022: 492–517; *ST* III, q.18). On most Catholic conceptions of God, there is no competition between creatures and God, such that an increase in causal power or perfection in one requires a decrease in the other. What is created can, and is meant to, entirely cooperate with God, but creatures do not lose their own powers and causality when they cooperate with, or participate in, God.

On the metaphysics of the seven earliest Councils, all things manifest themselves in acts according to the kind of thing they are, as St. John Damascene (676–749) and St. Thomas Aquinas explained (Damascene 1899: III, c.15; *ST* III, q.19, a.1). As we saw in Section 1, there is an *aesthetic* strain in the Catholic conception of God: God (and his revelation) is meant to be contemplatively perceived as holistic, pleasingly self-manifesting, good, and intelligible wholes – that is, as *beautiful* (Balthasar 2009). In the seventh century, the *monoenergists* held that Christ only had divine *activity, operation,* or *self-manifestation* (Greek *energeia*; Latin *operatio*), not human activity or self-manifestation. Even what Christ did with human powers was a divine activity, a manifestation of God. But again, this is to deny the full reality of Christ's humanity. Rather, God manifested himself in and through human nature. Everything that properly belongs to human beings belongs to Christ, including human activity and beauty. There are things that Christ did, like eating, sleeping, physically suffering, and being moved to joy or grief, which are human, not divine, activities. But even these activities are deified since it is a divine person who performs them, and these human activities subsist in that divine person. That Christ had both divine and human activities was affirmed at the Third Council of Constantinople.

Yet, this metaphysics leads to further problems regarding the Trinitarian God. First, if there is one activity per nature, then each person of the Trinity performs the same activity as each of the others since they have the same nature. The Father, the Son, and the Spirit have the same nature and so they perform the same activity and manifest themselves as one, aside from those activities that define the persons rather than manifesting the nature (such as the Father's act of begetting). For example, when God creates, each of the persons creates. Yet, there seem to be some acts that are not the person-constituting acts (like begetting) that only one person performs – for example, only the Son becomes incarnate. There seems to be a tension, if not a contradiction, between accounts of divine activities; more is needed on what a divine activity is. This problem was taken up in the Middle Ages, and I return to it in Section 3.

Second, given their shared activities, it is difficult to see how each divine person is a *person*, given widely held accounts of what it is to be a person. On conciliar metaphysics, a person is a concrete possessor of natures and acts. But as the term "person" has developed, especially after Rene Descartes (1596–1650) and John Locke (1632–1704), but also on Catholic scholastic and personalist philosophies, "person" refers to a subject or center of consciousness. To be an incommunicable possessor of intellectual and volitional nature and acts is to have one's acts of thinking, loving, and willing – that is, one's subjectivity or self-consciously grasped first-person point of view – as one's own. But if the three divine persons have one activity of thinking, loving, and willing in common, then it does not seem that they each are persons in this sense since they do not each have their own subjectivity. On that account, the divine persons appear like bare modes of the divine nature; in addition to seeming like a version of modalism, this view is difficult to reconcile with Scripture's portrayal of the distinctive character of each person. But if they each have their own incommunicable subjectivity, then it seems like we have three distinct sets of activities and, therefore, three instances of the divine nature, a view that is tantamount to tritheism.

On the solution to this problem given by some Catholic theologians, like Hans Urs von Balthasar (1905–88), the divine persons each have the one divine nature and activity but in a distinctive way. For example, the Father has the whole divine nature but as the one who begets, having the whole nature in an active and generative way, while the Son has the whole divine nature but as the one who is begotten, having it in a receptive way. Likewise, the persons each have the same activity, but they have it in distinctive ways: for example, the Father performs the act of creating in an initiating way, while the Son performs it in receptivity to the Father. In this way, their metaphysical unity, subjective incommunicability, and distinctive characters are all maintained (Balthasar 1998: 66–109). Similarly, some medieval theologians "appropriated" properties to each person: while each natural attribute and activity belongs to each person, we better grasp what is distinctive about each person by seeing affinities between a particular person and some attribute or activity. For example, there is an affinity between the Father and divine unity and the act of creation since the Father is the one source of the other persons and of all things; there is a distinct sense in which we call the Father "one" and "creator." On this view of divine attributes, each person has all the acts and attributes but in distinctive ways (*ST* I, q.39, a.8).

The seventh ecumenical council, the Second Council of Nicaea (787), developed the commitment to beauty and manifestation in Catholic conceptions of God. Building on oppositions to idolatry (inherited from the Jewish tradition) and to the material world (found in some Greek philosophy), those in the movement known as *iconoclasm* denied that Christ should be depicted in images. One worry they had was that, in depicting Christ, one would only depict his humanity, that which is visible and finite in him. His divinity, by contrast, is invisible and infinite, unable to be circumscribed in a finite image. To worship an image of Christ would then be idolatry since it would be worship only of a creature, Christ's humanity. But the council and Fathers like St. Theodore the Studite (759–826) responded that we can depict the *person* of Christ. When we look at another or at their image, we primarily see a *person*, not a nature. By taking on human nature, the Son made the person that he is able to be depicted. To say otherwise is to separate the natures into distinct *hypostaseis* (as on Nestorianism) or to deny the reality of Christ's human nature (as in Docetism). To worship an image of Christ is to worship the person of Christ. An image or icon participates in the *hypostasis* it depicts; like a Sacrament, it efficaciously conveys our attention to the one it depicts. Once again, the incarnate presence of God extends into the world (D 600–03; Theodore 1981; Pfau 2022: 127–219).

On this conception, God is present not only through images of Christ but also through saints, images of saints, and physical things associated with saints like relics of their body parts or clothing. As we have seen since Section 1, Catholics conceive of God as mediated to us through creatures, and our approach to him can be mediated through them. This is because creatures have all their properties through participation in God, especially through the primary point of creaturely mediation of God in Jesus Christ. When one thing participates or shares in another, the latter is a cause of the former. On the broadly Platonic and Aristotelian metaphysics that have been incorporated into the Catholic tradition, causes are present in their effects, and effects can convey a knower's attention to their causes. Because of this mediating structure of all creation and especially of those creatures who are most like God, it is appropriate to seek saints' intercession for needs, especially when these fall under their patronage. God's providential action is also conceived as mediated through their action and patronage, even in the case of miracles, which Catholics conceive as generally happening not only through divine omnipotence but also through creaturely mediation. Since God is present in images of Christ and saints, it is appropriate to worship God by bowing to them, kissing them, burning incense before them, laying flowers before them, or dressing them in liturgical vestments, as is done with the popular devotion to the statue of the Infant Jesus of Prague. Such worship is also appropriate with physical symbols of Christ, like crosses or the Easter candle. Because of the hypostatic union, physical things share in deification, and we share in deification through our liturgical and devotional engagement with them. Christ became a whole human being, body and soul, and we are redeemed, deified, and meant to relate to him with all that we are, not just interiorly.

Because of the Incarnation, the way one conceives of God is affected by how one conceives of human nature and created being in general; theology cannot be done apart from metaphysics and anthropology. Problems in those disciplines lead to problems regarding one's conception of God, and vice versa. We need to grasp what is included in human nature to understand who Christ is, and yet it is Christ who fully reveals what perfectly belongs to human nature (D 4322). As we have seen, a problem raised by the conciliar conception of God is the question of what belongs to human nature in itself, and what in human nature is compatible with assumption by a divine person. We have seen that, on the Catholic conception, sinfulness does not belong to human nature, but the Catholic tradition also has generally held that Christ knew all things about the world, not just with his divine mind but even with his human mind. This is because one person, the Son, has both minds and intellectual powers, and his human mind shares in the divine mind as perfectly as a human mind can (*ST* III, q.10–12).

These claims, which fit with the conciliar conception of Christ, lead to the following dilemma. If Christ did not experience the limitations of existing at a particular place and time, including ignorance, doubt, cultural prejudices, feelings of abandonment by God, and so forth, then it does not seem true that God took on the actual human condition. The Son then seems to lack some solidarity with, and mercy for, human beings, and something like Docetism would be true. But if Christ did experience human limitations, then either his divinity changed, such that he lost omniscience and other divine attributes, or his human and divine experiences were isolated from one another, so that he only experienced these limitations in his human nature. But the former is irreconcilable with classical theism, and the latter would entail that there are effectively two subjects in Christ, which is Nestorianism. Versions of the latter view are held by some of those Catholic Biblical scholars who distinguish the historical Jesus from the Christ of faith. Some have contended that Jesus, as represented in the Gospels, is a mere man, albeit one with a strong experience of God; on such a view, either Christ's humanity is experientially isolated from his divinity (which is a form of Nestorianism) or Christ was just a man, and the idea that he is God is an invention of the tradition (which is a form of adoptionism or Arianism) (Balthasar 1992: 173–208; Rausch 2003).

While the main lines of the Catholic tradition exclude these views, the problem remains as to how God can be conceived as both taking on the full human condition and as always fulfilling the classical theist account of God. The Catholic tradition has solved this problem by conceiving of human nature as allowing us to know and feel things in many distinct ways: because we have many powers and our powers can be actualized in different kinds of acts, a human being can be simultaneously ignorant of something in one way, while aware of it in another. This allows Christ to be ignorant of things in one way (by knowledge gained through the senses) but know all things in another way (by a higher awareness, informed by his divinity, sometimes called "infused knowledge") (*ST* III, q.10–12, q.46, a.7–8). Both the limitations of particular places and times, and the openness to transcendence of those limitations through participation in the divine, belong to human nature. In the words of the Second Vatican Council (1962–65), Jesus Christ fully reveals human beings to themselves, not vice versa (D 4322). The truest human condition is the condition of deification; the glory or full revelation of God is in deified human beings. The Son can take on the full human condition, indeed, the condition of a criminal and a slave, with its ignorance and negative feelings (though without sin) but simultaneously consciously reveal divinity through that condition. Similarly, the Catholic tradition conceives of God as revealed largely through Scripture but conceives of Scripture as having multiple layers of meaning. Just as Christ's humanity is conceived as being joined to divinity, likewise are the human words of Scripture, by the presence of God in them, made the instrument of divine self-revelation. In addition to the literal meaning of the text, which is in part discovered through historical research and includes the cultural symbols and beliefs of its writers, there are its deeper moral, Christological, and eschatological meanings: each text of Scripture allegorically reveals something about Christ, our moral and spiritual lives, and the last things, like heaven and hell (de Lubac 1998a; CCC 115–19).

2.3 The Trinity and the Image of God

I close this section by considering one development of the conciliar conception of God in medieval Western Catholicism. Scripture says that human beings are made in (or "according to") the image of God (*Genesis* 1:26–27). Since Christ is the full image of God, we image God insofar as we are like him (*Colossians* 1:15); again, his deified humanity is the paradigm for our humanity. Since human persons are in the image of God, we love God through loving other human persons; just as artistic images of God refer to God, so can love expressed to human persons be referred to God. The imperative to serve our neighbor is central to the way in which Catholicism conceives of God. God is not just to be conceived of speculatively but practically and ethically: God is the one who calls us to goodness, and this call reaches us, in part, through the image of God perceived in ourselves and others (Spencer 2018).

The image of God in us has been conceived in at least two ways; each of these conceptions is also a development of how the Trinity is conceived, though each also highlights problems with the Trinitarian conception of God. In devising the first conception of the image of God, St. Augustine (354–430) noted that all things resemble God, but only we human beings are said to bear an "image" of God. He finds in the structure of our mental activities not just an image of God's perfections but of the Trinity itself. Like the divine nature, the human mind or soul is simple, immaterial, immortal, free, and intelligent. Our mind performs three kinds of acts; we can see how the mind images the Trinity by considering how it performs these kinds of acts in relation to God. These acts can become an icon, referring our attention to God. We first "remember" God, that is, he comes to mind as something we previously implicitly grasped, say, in our longing for happiness. We express or articulate the content of that memory in a word or concept. Having articulately grasped God, we are then moved to willing love for him. Yet, these three acts – remembering, intellectually expressing, and loving will – are one with the mind. Similarly, the Father begets the Son as his Word, perfectly expressing what he is and, in begetting the Son, the act of love that is the Spirit proceeds. In both cases, three things are one in being. The more the human mind knows and loves God, the more it images or is like unto him, and so reveals him (Augustine 2002: 57–9, 142–50).

During the Middle Ages, the Trinitarian relations were increasingly conceived as matching this psychological account of human mental acts. On that view, the Son proceeds specifically from the divine intellect: in knowing himself, the Father naturally begets the Son or Word, as the expression of his self-knowledge. Likewise, the Spirit naturally proceeds from the divine will: in loving each other freely and willingly, the Father and the Son breathe forth the Spirit, the fruit of their love. That spiritual beings like us have just two basic ways of internally expressing themselves – intellectual expression and expression of love – explains why, in God, the supreme spiritual being, there are just two "expressions," two persons who proceed from the Father (Bonaventure 1882: 195–8; Cross 2005: 153–64; *ST* I, q.41). Once again, conceptions of created and divine persons are closely bound up with each other.

More recent theologians, including St. Theresa Benedicta of the Cross (Edith Stein) (1891–1942) and Pope St. John Paul II (1920–2005), have explored how the image of God is revealed in the human body. Knowledge and love of God are oriented to being expressed in the body, thereby enabling others to perceive and respond ethically to us as images of God (Stein 2002: 462–6). By the acts that are part of the image of God in us, we are oriented to give ourselves to God through knowledge and love. This orientation to self-gift and to communion among persons is also found in the structures of the human body: for example, in the way that male and female bodies are naturally ordered to give themselves to one another sexually in order to achieve marital unity and beget new persons (John Paul II 2005: 162–5, 176–81, 214) or in the way that any human body is naturally ordered to give itself in labor in order to build up society and the cosmos in imitation of God's creativity (John Paul II 1981b: 4, 6, 25).

In the Middle Ages, these sorts of considerations led to a second, social, rather than psychological, way of conceiving the image of God in us. Theologians like Richard of St. Victor (d. 1173) and Bonaventure noted that perfect personal acts like love and joy must be shared to be complete, and if they are shared only by two, they are insular and imperfect: their perfection requires sharing among at least three persons. In these experiences and the communities that they produce, which reveal love and joy to be perfections, we find an image that reveals why God must be three persons. To be the fullness of perfection, as classical theism conceives him, God must be an act of love and joy, but that requires him to be at least three persons (Richard of St. Victor 1855: 949–61; Bonaventure 1882: 57–8; Spencer 2022c).

Both here and in the psychological image, we see examples of the analogical reasoning that characterizes many Catholic conceptions of God (which will be considered further in Section 4). We reason from the limited existence of perfections in creatures to their absolute existence in God; limited perfections are conceived as participating in absolute and unlimited perfections. But problems arise in the tension between these two accounts of the image of God in us. As we have seen, neither divine nature nor divine personhood should be privileged over the other, on the Catholic conception of God. Using the psychological image of God, the divine persons could be seen as acts inhering in a shared nature, a view that emphasizes nature over personhood, with its attendant danger of modalism. Focusing on this image could lead to an anthropology that emphasizes individual mental acts as the primary way we approach and resemble God, as opposed to approaching God through communities, *eros*, the body, or nonmental acts. Using the social image of God, the divine persons could be seen as individuals in their own right, a view that emphasizes personhood over nature, with its attendant danger of tritheism. Focusing on this image could lead to an anthropology that sees individual persons as having importance not in themselves but only through communal relations. Both images present the danger of reductionistically emphasizing one aspect of personal life and participation in God over others and the danger of relating to God in an anthropomorphic way. The problem of how to conceive of God adequately will be considered again in Section 4, but, for now, we must note that the images must correct one another to have full theological value.

Having grasped Catholic conceptions of God as Trinitarian and as incarnate in Christ, I now turn to how God is conceived to relate to creation, and some problems that arose regarding that relation in the high Middle Ages.

3 Problems with God's Relations to Creatures

Catholic conceptions of God were shaped, especially during and just after the Middle Ages, by debates over relations between God and creatures. Many of these debates have no official, magisterial solution; rather, current Catholic conceptions of God are shaped by ongoing grappling with them. This section focuses on controversies regarding God's relations to, and actions toward, creatures, while Section 4 considers debates regarding creatures' relations back to God. I begin with God's actions toward creatures because, on any Catholic conception, God always takes the initiative in seeking human beings, rather than human beings first seeking God. After describing the Catholic conception of God as creator, I consider problems regarding God's providence and God's actions in themselves.

3.1 Metaphysics of Creation

On the Catholic conception, God creates the world "out of nothing" (*ex nihilo*) (D 3002). This excludes any *pantheism* on which the world is created "out of God," in the sense that the world *is* God, a part of God, or *only* a manifestation of God. Since God is simple, exists necessarily, and is goodness itself, and since creatures have these perfections only through participation in God's perfections, it follows that they are distinct in being from God. Unlike the Trinitarian persons, who have the same nature and are related to one another by natural or noncontingent processions, creatures are caused in a contingent divine act of willing. The Catholic conception of God as creator also excludes views on which some feature of creatures, like the matter out of which they are made, exists independently of causal dependence on God. Rather, everything distinct from God is dependent on God's creative causality. This is based on a general principle, drawn from classical metaphysics, which we have already seen, that everything imperfect depends on, and exists by sharing in, what is perfect (*ST* I q.65–66). God's creativity presupposes nothing apart from himself; hence, it is "creation *ex nihilo*."

God's sovereign creativity is attested by Scripture (e.g., *Genesis* 1–2) but is also grasped through philosophical arguments for his existence. Many such arguments have been widely accepted by Catholic thinkers. The First Vatican Council (1869–70) taught that we can grasp God's existence by reason, not just by faith (D 3004). We have already seen summaries of some such arguments, such as the Platonic argument in Section 1, on which we reason from the multiplicity of imperfectly unified and good entities to the perfect One and Good in which they participate for their unity and goodness, which we call God. What follows is my synthesis of a few other such arguments. Things around us are contingent: they do not explain their own existence or perfections. These must be explained by something other than themselves, which already has sufficient perfection to cause their perfections since nothing can cause a perfection that it does not already have in some way. On this view, the world is fully intelligible, that is, all things have a sufficient explanation. While contingent creatures and perfections are partially explained by the perfections and causal activity of other creatures, those other creatures do not fully account for them since their perfections also require explanation and a causal source. Given that the world is fully intelligible, there cannot be an infinite chain of creatures explaining and giving perfections and existence to one another. Were that the case, nothing would be thoroughly intelligible since the full explanation and source of existence would be infinitely deferred. Rather, there must be some first cause, which has all the perfections found in creatures, can cause perfection in others, and has these perfections with perfect unity, simplicity, and necessity, such that it does not require an explanation or causal source prior to itself. We call this absolutely perfect being, who is prior to all other beings, "God" (*ST* I q.2, a.3).

The Catholic tradition describes God's actions toward creatures using metaphysical language from the Platonic and Aristotelian traditions. The Church officially adopted this language, for example, at the Council of Vienne (1311–12) to describe the human soul's relation to the body, and at the Council of Trent (1545–63) to describe how Christ causes our redemption (D 902, 1529). On this metaphysics, to *cause* is to give actual existence to another, which occurs in several ways (Aquinas 1972). A creature's *material cause* (or matter) is that out of which it is made, that which potentially can be changed and actualized, that is, made definite and perfect. Its *formal cause* (or form) is the perfecting and actualizing principle that explains why its matter is unified into a persisting thing of some definite kind. For example, a human person's constantly changing matter is unified such that a person persists over time and is actually human, with human powers; the unifying principle that explains this is the *form* or *soul*. An *efficient cause* is what makes a thing or sustains it in existence; on the Catholic view, a human person's efficient cause is his or her parents and God since God is conceived as directly creating each human soul (*ST* I, q.90, a.2). A *final cause* is a thing's goal or purpose, that for the sake of which it exists; for us, this is union with God. An *exemplary cause* (or *formal exemplary cause*) is what a form shares in or imitates for its content. For example, a painting has its content because it imitates content in an artist's mind; that idea is its exemplary cause. Finally, an *instrumental cause* is something an efficient cause uses to bring about its effects; the efficient cause, often called the *primary cause*, uses the form and powers of the instrument, often called the *secondary cause*, to bring about some definite effect. For example, a writer uses a pen, with its form and powers, as an instrument to efficiently cause writing.

For the most part, Catholic thinkers have conceived of creation as a case of efficient causality: God makes creatures, including their matter and forms, to exist. God is also the final cause of human persons and of the whole cosmos. On many Catholic conceptions, something like *desire* (Greek *eros*; Latin *appetitus*) animates all things. Things are teleologically oriented to be like or to be united to God, though this does not benefit God by giving him new perfections. Rather, creation is sometimes understood as a gift of the divine persons to one another, where "gift" is something unnecessary and gratuitous, or as an act of self-gift by God to creatures (Balthasar 1998: 506–21). God's final causal role is often expressed aesthetically: creatures exist to praise or display God's glory, that is, to reveal his beauty or holistic self-manifestation, which includes all of his perfections (*ST* I, q.65, a.2; Balthasar 2009). Finally, God is the world's formal exemplary cause; creatures' formal content and perfections share in and imitate God's perfections and the content of his knowledge of the ways in which he can be imitated (which are called his "ideas"). Although creatures are not created "from God" in the sense of being made out of his substance, they are "from God," in that they have his formal content and perfections, and thereby share in his divinity (*ST* I, q.15).

3.2 Creation, Providence, and Predestination

We saw in Section 2 how, drawing on Augustine's psychological account of the image of God, medieval scholastics conceived of God as having the powers of intellect and will. As the efficient cause of human persons, God must have the perfections found in persons; given that our minds image God, God's acts and relations are analogous to those found in our minds. But medieval Catholic thinkers further debated how the powers of intellect and will are related, both in us and in God. This debate yielded a range of views between the extremes of *intellectualism* and *voluntarism* (Pinckaers 1995; Wolter 1997; Benedict XVI 2006; Hoffmann & Michon 2017). This debate led to further problems regarding how to conceive of God's acts toward creatures, like his act of creation. Differing views on this question arose in different religious orders, which are groups of men and women vowed to a life of religious devotion centered around a particular type of service or spirituality. Different orders, with distinct spiritualities, often have somewhat different conceptions of God; fruitful problems and tensions are thereby introduced into Catholic conceptions of God.

Intellectualism was emphasized by many in the Order of Preachers, a religious order founded by St. Dominic (1170–1221) and generally called the Dominicans, which largely adopted the theology of St. Thomas Aquinas, who was one of their early members. On intellectualism, we make acts of will based on what we intellectually grasp: once we know or believe that some action is best or ought to be done, we choose to do it. The *intellect* is our power to cognize any being; the *will* is our power to love and pursue any good. Human perfection is reached in an intellectual act, seeing God; our most perfect act is not an act of willing or loving, though it is aided by such acts. By analogy, God's act of creation is fundamentally intellectual: God wills to create what he intellectually judges as fitting or good among the ways that he can be manifested or imitated (which are, again, called his "ideas"). Creation manifests divine intellectual ideas, judgments, and perfections. We can reason from the structure of creation to at least some of the content of the divine mind. When God wills to reveal the moral law to us, for example, it describes what is actually fulfilling for our nature, which has its content through participation in God's ideas and perfections, which belong to him by nature. Creation reveals what God is like or God's character (*ST* I q.14, 15, 19; I–II, q.94, 98).

Voluntarism was emphasized by many in the Franciscan orders, which were founded by St. Francis (1181–1226) and St. Clare of Assisi (1194–1253) and which later adopted the theology of some of their members, such as St. Bonaventure, Bl. John Duns Scotus (1265–1308), and William of Ockham (1285–1347). On this view, what we will is not entirely determined by our intellectual understanding. Even after we have grasped all the reasons for an action, we must still choose what we do, and we can choose contrary to what we take to be our best reasons. On this view, our perfection is attained in an act of willing love for and enjoyment of God; we understand in order to love. On this view, God's act of creation is understood primarily as an act of will. Nothing about God's understanding or ideas – which are of all possible beings – sufficiently determines what God will create, and anything God could possibly create, which includes anything nonself-contradictory, would reflect his nature. On some versions of this view, like that of Scotus, God's loving will – and any act of will – have their own nonarbitrary order, albeit not one determined by the rationally graspable nature of things (Scotus 1954: 303–11; Wolter 1997: x–xi, 55–6; Scotus 2007: 130–1; Hoffmann 2013). On other versions of this view, like that of William of Ockham, God could have willed to give any moral law to us, regardless of whether it corresponded to our nature. God is not constrained by what is fitting, nor can we reason from the nature of creatures to what is fitting in God's judgment or to the content of his character. Rather, in creation and in giving a moral law, we just see God's free, loving generosity (William of Ockham 1981: 350–8).

Both views draw on the classical Aristotelian and Platonist traditions, which received significant attention from Catholic thinkers in the high Middle Ages. But intellectualism emphasizes Platonism's focus on the participation of imperfect individuals in what is transcendent and perfect, while voluntarism emphasizes Aristotelianism's focus on the distinctive causality and existence of individuals. As with many debates in Catholic tradition, this one is partly motivated by the problem of how to synthesize potentially conflicting older traditions. If intellectualism is true, then it is hard to see how God or created persons are free, that is, self-determining and able to select among alternative known possibilities. Rather, all acts of will seem determined by intellectual judgments; since God is omniscient, then it would seem that he must create the most fitting world. Creation seems to then be necessary, contrary to how it appears and to how Catholicism conceives of it as God's *free* gift (D 4102). Voluntarism safeguards God's freedom, but it makes it difficult to know what God is like: we can know *that* God created all things and *what* God reveals, but we cannot reason to what he judges to be most fitting or to the content of his character. There is a danger that we will see God's choices, including his choice to create or to prescribe a moral law, as arbitrary, and thereby conceive of God as fundamentally characterized as pure power, rather than as good, loving, generous, and trustworthy.

A plausible solution to this problem must see the act of creation as simultaneously intellectual, fitting, and free, that is, as an act of love that freely aims at what is beautiful or fitting. Each of the thinkers mentioned earlier seeks a solution like this; yet, given their emphases, their views can easily be taken as fitting with the problematic results just discussed. This debate affects many aspects of Christian moral, liturgical, and devotional life, and it affects how we conceive of God's decision to create and become incarnate. Intellectualism and some versions of voluntarism lead to seeing the Christian life as consisting of developing our nature in virtue so as to participate in what fits with human and divine nature. God decides to create, become incarnate, and deify in order to share his nature with others. However, on some such views, he does this only in response to our sinfulness (*ST* III, q.1, a.3), while on other views, he would have become incarnate regardless of whether we sinned since his purpose in creating was always to deify us, and this requires the joining of natures found in the Incarnation (Dean 2006; Scotus 2006: 284–91). In each case, he became incarnate because it was the most fitting thing for love to do. More extreme versions of voluntarism, by contrast, lead one to see the Christian life as consisting of obeying laws decreed by God positivistically and perhaps arbitrarily. God contingently decreed a moral law, became incarnate because that moral law required punishment for sin, and then decided to take on that punishment himself. On this conception, it is hard to see why God does these things since he could have decreed some other moral law, which did not require such extreme punishment. The struggle between these views has shaped Catholic moral and spiritual experience since the Middle Ages (Pinckaers 1995).

On most Catholic views, God not only causes things to exist at their first moment but also conserves or sustains them in existence at all moments. Most scholastic metaphysics hold that some distinction can be drawn between a being's *existence*, its being distinct from nothing and from its causes, and its having actual perfection, and its *essence*, the content of what the being is (Suárez 1861: 224–8). No creaturely essence necessitates its actual existence at any moment; rather, creatures must continually receive existence, ultimately from God. But scholastics debated whether creatures receive actualities other than existence, like their actions, *directly* from God. The Catholic tradition excludes views like *occasionalism* on which God is the only cause of all creaturely actualities, including their actions; we saw in Section 2 how conciliar Christology requires created natures to have their own powers and activities, distinct from God's.

Most medieval scholastics held a view now called *concurrentism*, on which a creature's actions are caused both by that creature and by God. God must directly cause actions along with the creature for three reasons. First, every creaturely actuality, including exercises of powers, has content through participation in God, and no creature could share in God unless that participation were given by God. Second, acts exist as having some kind, and if God is the source of the act's existence, he must also cause the content of its kind, for this is the content of its existence. Third, Catholics have, in general, held to a strong view of *providence*, God's awareness and guiding of the course of the history of the cosmos and of each thing. God watches over and cares for each thing and ensures that they reach the final state he has willed for them. Concurrentists hold that this requires God to have direct causal control over every event (Garrigou-Lagrange 1937; Freddoso 1994). I present here some varieties of concurrentism that are developments of medieval views, which were developed in part in response to strands of Protestantism on which God acts upon us without any possibility of our resistance or cooperation (D 1554–7).

One view, held by many Dominicans and other followers of St. Thomas Aquinas, is often called Bañezianism, after the Dominican theologian Domingo Bañez (1528–1604). God causes creatures' acts by introducing into creatures an actuality, a "physical premotion," by which they cause themselves to perform exactly that act that God wills. God is related to each creature, including us, as primary, efficient cause to instrumental, secondary cause. By his "premotion," God directly causes everything about each action, aside from any lack of goodness it has; for example, God does not cause the sinfulness of sinful acts since their sinfulness consists of a lack of goodness they ought to have. The sinfulness of a sinful act comes from the creature performing the act, while the positively existing features of the act come from both God and the creature. When a premotion to act well is introduced into a morally defective subject, a sinful action is produced. God does not directly cause sinfulness and other lacks, but he willingly permits them. By premoving each creature to each of its acts, God has providence over every event and over the course of history. Our acts remain free here inasmuch we cause them on the basis of reasons, using a power by which we determine ourselves and by which we can act otherwise than we do (Bañez 1585: 515; Garrigou-Lagrange 1946b: 256–65, 293–4, 319–23; Spencer 2016: 386–8).

Another view, held by many in the Society of Jesus or Jesuit order (founded by St. Ignatius of Loyola [1491–1556]), is known as Molinism, after the Jesuit theologian Luis de Molina (1535–1600). This view, like Bañezianism, was meant to be an interpretation of Thomas Aquinas' texts. Beginning around the fifteenth century, Western Catholic theology and philosophy increasingly relied on Thomas' texts. Many Catholic debates were not only about what is true but also about how to interpret those texts. This became even more the case during the late nineteenth century, when Pope Leo XIII (1810–1903) mandated the use of Thomas' texts in Catholic seminaries and schools (Leo XIII 1879). On Molinism, God and a creature each co-cause the creature's act, but God does not directly move the creature to its act; the creature is not God's instrument since that is incompatible, on this view, with creaturely freedom. Rather, they are simultaneous efficient causes of the one act. God gives the creature enough causal power such that it acts as it wishes, and then God bestows existence on the act that the creature selects. Although God does not directly cause each event, he still has providence over all events because he knows what each creature would do were it in any possible situation. By guiding the course of which situations come about, and thereby ensuring that creatures select only those acts that he wills, God maintains providential control over what occurs (de Molina 1595: 202–8; Perszyk 2012; Spencer 2016: 396–7).

There are other concurrentist theories (Garrigou-Lagrange 1946b: 112–16, 153–82), but a major debate among Catholic thinkers, the *de auxiliis* controversy (1581–1611), arose between Bañezians and Molinists. Bañezianism is one of a larger family of Thomistic views (Spencer 2016: 385–98) on which God is the transcendent, primary cause of all things, the source of all goodness and causality, who works in every secondary cause. Secondary causes are genuine causes, albeit causes by participation in God's causality, which enables, and is not in competition with, every other kind of causality; God transcends and is the source of all modes of creaturely causality, whether necessary, contingent, or free. The world with all its details is, on this view, the unfolding and revealing of content that preexists in God, though God always transcends his self-revelation in the world. Molinism, by contrast, is one of a family of modern views that hold that, while God is the primary cause and ultimate source of all causality, he could not determine what we do without that eliminating our freedom. Rather, God must give us freedom by giving us exclusive causal control over our acts and withdrawing his own causal influence. The underlying debate here is rooted in the contrast between the Greek and Jewish views of God. If we emphasize that God is goodness itself (even if we also hold that God is an individual agent) and is to be understood as something like a Platonic Form, in which creatures participate, then it makes sense to hold, with the Bañezians, that God is a transcendent cause of our acts and that his causality does not compete with or diminish our own causality. But if we emphasize that God is a free and intelligent individual agent (even if we also hold that God is something like the Platonic Form of goodness itself), who makes definite judgments and choices, then his free decisions could be in competition with ours. It then makes sense to hold, with the Molinists, that God must restrict his causal influence to allow for ours. Inasmuch as Catholic conceptions of God maintain that he is both transcendent goodness *and* a free individual agent, it is subject to the tension between these views.

While these versions of concurrentism are conceptions of how God causes *any* creaturely act, the *de auxiliis* controversy focused on God's gift of grace, the deifying participation in his life that enables us to perform divine or supernatural acts, like acts of charity or loving others entirely for God's sake, acts that exceed what we can do through our natural powers alone. We saw in Section 1 how the Catholic conception of God excludes *Pelagianism*, on which we can merit and achieve the life of deification or grace by our own natural efforts. Rather, God must give us any share in his life and in the saving acts of Christ that we receive (D 1528–30). However, once we share in his life, we can merit further grace by acting in virtue of it – that is, one act of cooperatively participating in God's loving life can lead to deeper participation in that life (*ST* I–II, q.114; D 1545–6). The *de auxiliis* controversy was, in large part, over when and to whom God gives grace; it is a debate over *predestination*, the act by which God elects a person to receive grace or the glory of being with him eternally (Garrigou-Lagrange 1946b; Spencer 2016; O'Neill 2019). Since any share in God's life is a gift from God, it can only be received if God takes the initiative to give it; God must "destine" persons to receive grace prior to their receiving it. How we conceive of predestination affects how we conceive of God's knowledge of creation and of his love and mercy toward us.

Building upon one interpretation of St. Augustine and St. Thomas Aquinas (especially Augustine 1887b and *ST* I q.22–23), all Bañezians and many Molinists held that God predestines some, but not all, persons to receive grace and attain union with him – colloquially, to "be saved" or "go to heaven" (Garrigou-Lagrange 1946b: 183–232). On many versions of these views, most people do not go to heaven. God elects the saved prior to any consideration of the goodness of their acts. Persons perform good, meritorious acts only because they first are given grace. With the Council of Trent (D 1554), all parties to this debate hold that we can resist God's offer of grace: God does not deify us without our cooperation (Augustine 1992: 231). But different groups understand this claim in different ways. On this first view, on which God predestines people "prior to foreseen merits," God offers grace to everyone, but he only gives the aid needed to accept that grace to some persons (see *Matthew* 22:14). Those to whom he does not give that aid – those whom he "negatively reprobates" or willingly permits to "go to hell" – resist his offer of grace and so are ultimately permanently separated from him. This view emphasizes God's free sovereignty, the idea that the world in all its details is a manifestation of divine perfection and will, the unknowability of God's reasons for electing some persons, and the radical dependence of all creatures on his will. It seeks to account for the experiences, rooted in the Jewish tradition, of being elected or called by God to a life of holiness and to a particular vocation or mission in life, and of observing that some other persons apparently do not experience such a call.

The view that many people do not attain deification is held here despite the Scriptural and conciliar claims that God wills all to be saved and that Christ died for all people (*1 Timothy* 2:4; *1 John* 2:2; D 1522) and despite the Catholic devotional and liturgical prayers that ask God to save all persons (such as the "Fatima prayer" often said with the Rosary or the Good Friday intercessions in the Roman Mass). To reconcile these views, those who hold this view distinguish God's absolute or antecedent will and power from his ordained or consequent will and power (*ST* I q.19, a.6, ad1). By the former, God wills ends apart from considering particular events; at this abstract level, he wills that all be deified and he died for all people. But, taking into account the particulars of this world, God wills that the cosmos reveal him as perfectly as possible. Given this goal, it is better (the view claims) that many not be saved or receive the effects of Christ dying for them, so that every kind of good may be represented in the cosmos, including goods like the manifestation of his justice.

This view of predestination was rejected by some Molinists and by some outside the two sides of the *de auxiliis* debate, including many in the Eastern tradition. They argue that the former view seems incompatible with divine goodness and justice because God is ultimately responsible for sin and damnation on this view since, had he given the requisite grace, sins would not have occurred; he cannot justly both withhold the necessary aid and punish persons for doing what could only have been done with that aid. Some, like St. Francis de Sales (1567–1622), held that God "predestines" people to heaven only because of the good, meritorious acts he knows that they will perform through cooperation with grace. God's election is not arbitrary or inscrutable but is based on persons' actual acts of cooperating with grace (de Sales 1997: 141–3). Some personalists, including some of the fathers of the Second Vatican Council (D 4324), building on both Thomas Aquinas (1961: c.112–13) and post-Kantian philosophy, argue that, because of their being made in the image of God, because of their power for free self-determination and self-gift, and because they are ordered toward deification, human persons are created by God for their own sake, and so have value and dignity in themselves. For this reason, it is always wrong to use a person as a means to an end. God *could not* justly will any person's damnation, even by merely permitting it, as a means to any end, including revealing his own attributes. Rather, on this view, the only appropriate response to a person is love; since he is love, God would offer grace and the possibility of deification to all persons, and all persons would be able to freely accept or reject that offered grace (John Paul II 1981a: 21–44; Crosby 1996: 65–72, 239–43; Spencer 2016).

Those who hold this view could also hold that God only absolutely predestines Christ (and perhaps Mary) to deification but offers all others a share in that predestination through participation in Christ's body, the Church (Balthasar 1992: 282–4; Dean 2006). Balthasar and others have argued that this view, coupled with a strong view of God's mercy manifested in Christ and a trust in God's ability to providentially lead all things to the greatest manifestation of his goodness, should lead us to confidently hope that all persons, and even the whole cosmos, will be deified (Balthasar 1998: 269–321; Benedict XVI 2007: n.46–7). Scriptural texts that seem to guarantee damnation for some (e.g., Lk. 13:22–30) should be read allegorically as moral warnings, which need not literally be fulfilled. However, historically, this view was rejected by the great majority of theologians.

In the *de auxiliis* controversy, many Bañezians worried that Molinism amounted to a form of Pelagianism. Many Molinists worried that Bañezianism is tantamount to forms of Calvinist Protestantism rejected by the Church on which God directly wills even sins, thereby positively predestining certain people to hell, a view inconsistent with the Catholic conception of human freedom. But the result of the controversy was that Pope Paul V (1550–1621) ruled that both views were consistent with Catholic doctrine (D 1997). The upshot of this is that Catholics conceive of God through the tensions produced by this debate; they seek to balance strong views of divine and human freedom, while affirming divine justice, generosity, and goodness.

Beyond the concurrentist parties to these debates, a view, sometimes tendentiously called *mere conservationism*, arose among some medieval Franciscans, like Peter John Olivi (1248–1298) (Freddoso 1994; Frost 2014). Popularly, it is now a very widespread view among Catholics. On this view, God conserves (or continually gives existence to) substances but does not need to cause their actions; rather, he gives creatures enough power to cause their own actions without his direct concurrence. This can be joined to the view on which God offers grace to all persons. Unlike the concurrentist, the mere conservationist need not hold that God wills evil acts in any sense, even permissively. This view allows for complete, self-determining freedom in created persons, and for other creaturely events (like evolutionary events) to occur without direct divine causality or design. (It should be noted that most contemporary Catholics, given traditional allegorical ways of reading Scripture, see no conflict between the claim that God is the ultimate cause and conserver of all things and evolutionary claims about the origins of biological species [Austriaco 2019].) But this does not remove God's providence: An omniscient God knows how he will respond to any possible event and he directly sees all events; God can guide history to his intended ends by specially intervening at particular moments in history (Balthasar 1990a: 278).

But while this conception of God's relations to creatures allows for a more straightforward affirmation of creaturely freedom and divine goodness, it runs into problems regarding divine knowledge and responsiveness. If God does not cause creaturely acts, then it is hard to see how he can know them. On concurrentism, God knows what occurs not by receiving information from the world (since he is impassible, and so cannot be causally acted on by creatures) but by knowing what he wills to cause or permit. Since God does not will creaturely acts on mere conservationism, he cannot know them that way. But it also seems that he cannot know them by observing them since, again, he is impassible, and observation seems to require that one receive something from the observed object. Likewise, it is hard to see how God could be responsive to prayer or other creaturely acts on mere conservationism. Responsiveness seems to require that God acts *because of* a creaturely act. On concurrentism, creatures pray because God wills and causes them to do so, and then God responds to the prayer because he wills it; petitionary prayer, on that view, is a matter of creatures participating in God's giving of goodness to the world (*ST* II–II, q.83, a.2). Mere conservationism cannot make sense of petitionary prayer in that way since God does not cause creaturely acts on that view, but neither can God be actualized by creatures since he is impassible. It seems that, as with divine knowledge, mere conservationism cannot make sense of petitionary prayer at all. But concurrentism has parallel problems: God's willing and knowing of the actual world must be contingent acts since their object could have not existed and other things could have existed instead. But saying that God performs contingent acts seems inconsistent with divine simplicity since performing contingent acts seems to involve taking on acts one would otherwise not have performed, that is, entering into composition with new acts. Seeing how the Catholic tradition dealt with these problems requires considering how it has conceived of divine action.

3.3 Divine Action

Both Eastern and Western Christian traditions have grappled with the problem of how to conceive of divine action. A successful conception will explain how God knows and wills actual, contingent creation, and how an impassible God can respond to creaturely acts, including prayers. Furthermore, it will explain religious experiences in which someone experiences just one divine attribute, such as God's wrath or mercy. Since God is simple, it would seem that he cannot manifest just one attribute apart from the others (Farges 1926).

According to much of the Thomistic tradition, God is perfectly, eternally, and timelessly actual, and so is no different regardless of whether he creates or what he creates. Everything contingent in divine action is found outside of God. In himself, God is eternally the same act of willing, knowing, and loving himself. His willing, knowing, and loving of contingent creatures consists of those creatures considered in their dependence on him (Spencer & Grant 2015). While creatures are "really related" to God, that is, their relation to him involves changes in them and dependence on him, God only has "relations of reason" to creatures, that is, his relations to creatures do not involve anything contingent or changeable in him, but rather all the change involved in his contingent acts is found in the creatures who depend on and are present to him (*ST* I q.13, a.7). This model emphasizes that all divine attributes are one in being. Even on that model, though, we are correct to make distinctions about God's attributes; God really is both just and merciful, for example, but "justice" and "mercy" do not mean the same thing, even though divine justice and mercy are one in being. All the perfection found in creaturely justice and mercy is first in God but in an entirely unified way. God necessarily has many ideas about how he can be participated by creatures, in virtue of which he makes and is present to distinct creatures (*ST* I, q.13, a.4; q.15).

One might object that Scripture, tradition, and experience show God to be responsive and intimately present to us and that this is not captured by this Thomistic view. One response is that philosophical discoveries about God – like divine simplicity and immutability – constrain how we interpret Scripture and experience. The latter are taken literally when reconcilable with the former, but as metaphorically otherwise, though metaphors can be taken to express deeper truths about God than literal claims. Manifestations of God, like grace, are creatures. They are effects of God that mediate his presence or the content of a divine attribute. They mediate his presence by resembling him in some way, but they are not literally God (*ST* I, q.1, a.9; I–II, q.110). One might worry that this account fits best with a view on which claims that God intimately loves us and is moved to mercy and compassion for us are just metaphors, not literally true. Likewise, to be deified, on this model, seems to be only a matter of taking on created effects that imitate God but not literally sharing directly in his life. This view also seems to not explain how God contingently causes creatures. Changes in effects extrinsic to a cause are normally explained by changes in that cause. But, on this view, God just directly causes creatures and, in himself, is the same regardless of whether or what he creates. It is hard to see how that explains why these contingent features of creatures exist rather than others.

Other Catholic thinkers proposed different conceptions of divine action and attributes. John Duns Scotus, along with other Franciscans, argue that, for the distinctions we make about God to be true and for us to be able to have experiences of distinct divine attributes, those attributes must be distinct in God. Scotus argues that a thing's attributes can be distinct, and ground distinct causal effects, even while being inseparable and one in being or perfection, a kind of distinction he called the "formal distinction" (Dumont 2005). That God has formally distinct attributes is consistent with God being simple, that is, lacking composition out of parts that are prior to him. On this view, God can act and manifest himself through just one attribute.

Many Jesuits argued that, while God cannot take on new *perfections* or *actualities*, this does not exclude him taking on new and contingent *experiences* or *intentional* (object-directed) *acts*, so long as these are manifestations of, not additions to, his perfection. There is contingency in God's acts of knowing, willing, and loving creatures in God, not just external to him. God can "see" what happens in some creaturely act without causing that act and without being causally affected by it because, on this view, an intelligent being grasps whatever is present to it when it has the idea of the object. Since God necessarily has the ideas of all possible beings and is causally present to all things, God can "see" or know all beings, without directly causing every aspect of them and without this violating his ontological impassibility. Likewise, God can thereby respond to beings: he can perform acts because creatures performed acts, like prayers, which he "sees." Responsiveness does not require that God be *causally* affected by creatures (that is, receive new perfections from creatures) but just that he be *intentionally* affected by them (that is, take on an object of his intentional acts that he would not otherwise have) and act on that basis. The Jesuit conception allows us to take Scriptural and experience-based claims about God's actions literally and thereby account for the full range of experiences of God (Suárez 1861: 127–30; Clarke 1994: 183–210).

While rejecting the Franciscan and Jesuit claims about distinctions in God, the Thomistic tradition nevertheless includes aspects of this conception of divine action. On Thomas' view, God is omnipresent by his general causal power. Since some things participate in or resemble God more perfectly than other things, God is more present to things that participate in him more (like persons) than to lower things (like inorganic things). But particular divine persons are also especially present in certain things. The Son *is* Jesus, and so is personally present there. The Eucharist is substantially Jesus, and so, again, the Son is personally present there. The Son is also present in distinctive ways in Scripture, those being deified, priests, the poor, and those who suffer. The Spirit is distinctively present in believers through his gifts, like wisdom or piety. In each of these cases, on Thomas' view, the Father "sends" the Son or the Spirit to a creature. These contingent "divine missions" are just the act by which the person proceeds eternally from the Father taking on a new object at which it aims. God eternally begets the Son, but when the Son is sent to me (say, at my baptism), I become an object of that act of begetting, on the Thomistic view. I am deified by being the object of the eternal Trinitarian acts: the Father begets me as he does the Son, so that I am an adopted son of God, a son within the Son, and, with the Spirit, the fruit of God's love (*ST* I, q.43; Balthasar 1990a: 308–12; Balthasar 1992: 191–208).

One further solution within the Catholic tradition to these problems about divine action comes from the Eastern Church. In Section 1, I discussed how in the Middle Ages there was a split between the Catholic Church and the Eastern Orthodox, though some of the latter subsequently returned to union with Catholicism. When they did so, they brought with them theologies that had developed in the East. How to integrate Eastern and Western theologies is a significant but fruitful problem in Catholicism.

Following the Third Council of Constantinople and the Second Council of Nicaea and building on the theology of St. Gregory Palamas (1296–1359), Eastern theology emphasizes the distinction between God's essence (*ousia*) and his activities or manifestations (*energeiai*). God includes activities or manifestations of what he essentially is. These include free activities, by which he makes himself present to creatures, much like the intentional acts proposed by the Jesuits. God's presence to us in grace, Sacraments, or religious experience is not just the presence of a created effect that resembles God but his literal presence through an act of self-manifestation. By sharing in and cooperating with these activities, creatures really share in his life, and thereby are deified (Palamas 1983).

As we can see, Catholic tradition has responded to problems regarding divine action by adopting various, flexible accounts of the simple, immutable God (Spencer 2017). I now consider how human relations to God affect our conception of him, and some of the problems that have arisen regarding our conception of those relations.

4 Problems with Human Approaches to God

This final section considers ways we relate to God, in response to his relations to us. There is great diversity among Catholic approaches to God, which leads to many potentially conflicting conceptions of God. I begin with a tension in Western Catholic spirituality between what I call "sacramental" and "mystical" approaches to God, which is partly rooted in the tension between the Greek and Jewish inheritances discussed in Section 1. We have seen that Catholicism includes multiple religious orders, many of which have differing spiritualities or approaches to spiritual life and practice. We have also seen that Catholicism approaches God sacramentally, through liturgy and other material realities, but that it has also often conceived of God as best approached through intellectual thought and by ascetically setting aside material things. These approaches have often been in tension. After considering spiritualities excluded by Catholic conceptions of God, I turn to spiritualities that are representative of this tension, emphasizing how their conceptions of God differ. I then consider problems regarding our *knowledge* of God and our *desire* for God. Given its great influence on current Catholic practice, that debate is a fitting place to close this Element.

4.1 Boundaries of Catholic Spirituality

Catholicism conceives of God as the creator of all things distinct from him and as one who has made possible the deification of everything in human persons (other than sin) through the incarnation. Views like *Manicheanism*, on which matter is fundamentally evil and the goal of human life involves freedom from matter, are excluded; since it is made by God, matter cannot be fundamentally evil (Augustine 1991: bk.5). We have also seen that Catholics conceive of God as one who shares perfections with others, including causal power and freedom. This excludes spiritualities like *Quietism*, on which one strives to be entirely passive to God's acts, without contributing one's free cooperation (D 2201–69). God, above all, shares himself with us through the Body of his Son, the extension of the Incarnation, which is the Catholic Church (D 4118–19). In other words, God is primarily present to us communally, through the Church's liturgies, Sacraments, and authoritative teachings, and through its people, especially the poor. Spiritualities on which the communal and concrete presence of God is entirely set aside in favor of private religious experience are excluded (Knox 1994). God manifests himself through this Church and its ritual acts on his own initiative: God is conceived as having promised to make himself present to us in the Sacraments, which will cause their effects so long as we do the work he has given us (*ex opere operato*). Contrary to *Donatism*, on which God makes himself present through rituals only because of the moral excellence of the minster, Catholicism conceives of God as making himself reliably present as a gift (D 1612; Augustine 1887a; Feingold 2021: 458, 466–75).

A range of spiritualities are compatible with these exclusions. To grasp how God is conceived throughout the Catholic Church, one must have a sense for this range of approaches and for the tensions and problems that thereby arise. We have already seen some of these tensions, for example, the tension (described in Section 3) between the Franciscan emphasis on will and affection in our approach to God, and the Dominican emphasis on the intellect.

4.2 Sacramental or Cataphatic Spirituality

The "sacramental" strand of spirituality, which conceives of God as present to us primarily through the mediation of material, sensible things, is "cataphatic," that is, it holds that we can speak positively about what and who God is. On some such spiritualities, we experience God through interior sensory experiences, like affections and acts of imagination. For example, on one spirituality of the Jesuit order, pioneered by St. Ignatius of Loyola, God makes himself present to us when we imagine ourselves with him in Biblical scenes. We can thereby approach the God who became incarnate and sensible; since God is providentially present in all things, he is present in our imagination, and we can speak positively of him on that basis (Ignatius 1999: xvi–xvii, 6–9).

Other such spiritualities focus on God's presence to us through external sensory experiences. We have seen how Sacraments, like Baptism and Eucharist, allow us to experience God and speak positively about his action in our lives. We have also seen how, through creation, God is revealed through each natural species and individual; at least on the intellectualist view, we can perceive God through the beauty and intelligibility of creatures, and we can reason from features of creatures to the content of God's ideas and perfections, and thereby speak positively about God. We also thereby grasp God as the one who calls us to safeguard the natural world; our role vis-à-vis the natural world is to act as priests, contemplating how creation speaks of God and sacrificially offering it back to God through how we enable it to imitate him more (Francis 2015; Spencer 2022b: 310–11).

Some Catholic spiritualities have focused on other external sensory experiences that allow us to speak positively about God. We saw in Section 1 that Catholicism inherited from the Jewish tradition the experience of God relating to his people (Israel, the Church) as a lover does to his bride (see, e.g., *Song of Songs*). Catholicism also inherited from the Greek tradition the experience of our desire for God being a form of *eros*, the sort of love that animates sexual attraction (see, e.g., Plato's *Symposium*). Some Catholic spiritual traditions, exemplified for example by St. Bernard of Clairvaux (1090–1153), a member of the Cistercian order, likewise emphasized that God relates to the Church, the whole People of God, as his bride, but he also relates to each person in this way, especially to the saints and most especially to Mary (de Lubac 1999: 353–64; Bernard of Clairvaux 1971–1980). There are aspects of God's love and happiness, and his orientation to share these with us, which are only grasped through experiences of affective union with him and which are adequately describable only with erotic metaphors. In contemporary times, a range of "theologies of the body" have conceived of God as revealed especially through marital experiences (Marion 2008; Johnson 2015; Hildebrand 2017; Waldstein 2021). Pope St. John Paul II emphasized how God's self-giving, interpersonal love is revealed through the orientation of the human body to be a gift for another in marital, sexual acts. Marriage is a Sacrament on the Catholic view; marriage, and the acts proper to it, are understood to distinctly make present the union between Christ and the Church (John Paul II 2005).

Many versions of both sacramental and mystical spirituality conceive of God as present to us through ascetic practices or suffering. Mystical spiritualities (discussed in the following) consider suffering and asceticism necessary to strip away ways of wrongly conceiving and relating to God and other persons. But many sacramental spiritualities grasp how we can speak positively of who God is on the basis of experiences of suffering. In the doctrine of the Incarnation, God is conceived as humbling or emptying himself, becoming a man and not appearing obviously as God, to unite us to himself (*Philippians* 2). God's self-giving, self-emptying love, the love among the Trinitarian persons, was especially manifested through his bloody death on the Cross; as we saw in Section 1, the Cross is taken by many Catholics to transform the evil status of suffering into a means to union with God. On many spiritualities, we only fully experience and imitate God's love – and, so, only have the union of love and will that is the most central feature of deification – by consciously joining our suffering to his, that is, by internalizing the experience of suffering along with him. This includes seeing any suffering we undergo as a gift from God, an opportunity to become like Christ in accepting God's will and living in a loving way through that suffering. This is certainly not a license to inflict suffering on others or fail to alleviate suffering. On the Catholic view, we ought to do all we can to alleviate others' suffering and seek justice for sufferings inflicted on us by other human persons. But when we suffer, we can view it as an opportunity to make, with Christ, an offering of our lives to God for the sake of making the world and ourselves more "at one" with him. These spiritualities are especially consonant with the theology, described in Section 3, on which God has providence over all things, in the sense of at least permitting all events and drawing good out of all events (De Caussade 2010). This aspect of the Catholic conception of God is evoked by practices like the Stations of the Cross and the Good Friday liturgy. It is graphically represented in the lives of saints like the martyrs who embraced and celebrated their own sufferings (CCC 2473–4), and of saints who have voluntarily taken on physical sufferings. For example, St. Gemma Galgani (1878–1903) frequently physically experienced something like Christ's scourging and crucifixion (including the appearance of Christ's wounds on her body, known as the "stigmata") and had visions of Christ asking her to share in his sufferings in this way (Germanus 2000).

Many cultures in which Catholicism has taken root have developed symbols and rituals for relating to and conceiving God. Often, these are rooted in a saint's experience of God or in an apparition of Jesus, Mary, or a saint – that is, an experience of one of these persons appearing to someone and revealing God in a way distinctive to that culture. Many of these conceptions incorporate aspects of cultures' non-Christian religious beliefs and practices. Some Catholics have conceived of God's self-revelation in various cultures and religions as participating in, and preparatory for, the full revelation of God in Christ; the Word is present in all cultures, preparing all for union with God (John Paul II 1994: 77–83). Catholicism's ability to incorporate symbols, liturgical elements, and ideas about God, the human person, and all of reality from each culture is of increasing importance as Catholicism flourishes more and more in the global South. This synthesizing with other cultures will surely lead to developments of the Catholic conception of God, but it will also likely lead to new philosophical problems having to do with God.

Finally, many Catholics, especially those in cultures who have suffered oppression, including some of those same cultures in the postcolonial global South, also conceive of God as a liberator not only from sin but also from concrete evils like hunger, racism, and political and economic hardship; God is revealed sacramentally through the struggle for social justice and through the defense of all human life (Gutiérrez 1988). Even if God *can* be encountered profoundly through suffering, God also wants us to alleviate others' sufferings and to ultimately encounter him just in positive ways. This is an experience of God rooted in the experience of the Old Testament prophets and summed up in Mary's hymn, the Magnificat (*Luke* 1:46–55). God is conceived positively as one who is concerned for the amelioration of the world not just eschatologically but in history too. However, when these are placed in tension, such that God is conceived *only* as a *temporal* deliverer, only as a motivator of social improvement, or as a being who himself develops toward a more perfect future state, such conceptions fall outside a Catholic conception of God (Congregation for the Doctrine of the Faith 1984). But although God ultimately calls us, on the

Catholic conception, to union with himself, more than to political liberation, God can only be fully conceived by experiencing the call to prefer the poor and vulnerable in individual and social action; God is conceived as the one who gives creation to all human persons and who calls us to ever more perfect justice (CCC 2402–3, 2448).

4.3 Mystical or Apophatic Spirituality

Other Catholic spiritualities are "apophatic" or theologically "negative," emphasizing how our images, words, and positive experiences fall short of conveying or grasping what and who God is; we are more able to say what God is *not* than what he positively is. The Fourth Lateran Council taught that for any likeness between God and creatures, there is an even greater unlikeness (D 806). Some contemporary Catholic philosophers, like Jean-Luc Marion, have argued that God cannot be captured in any creaturely category. If "being" and "cause" are categories into which finite creatures fall, then, given his transcendence, God is not a being or a cause but "beyond" causality and being; we best grasp God by denying of him what we include in those categories (Marion 1995).

Apophatic or "mystical" spiritualities emphasize the need to ascetically distance ourselves from aspects of material life in order to be deified. On the view of many in the tradition of the Carmelite religious orders, like St. John of the Cross (1542–91) and St. Teresa of Avila (1515–82), any love for creatures, except as a means to union with God, is idolatrous. Even though images and material things *can* guide us to greater closeness with God, any attachment to them must ultimately be set aside to attain union with God (Teresa of Avila 1989; John of the Cross 1991). Many in the early modern French spiritual tradition advocated abandoning ourselves to divine providence, accepting whatever happens to us as God's will, not passively or quietistically, but in the sense of cooperating with whatever providence sends. Similarly, in the medieval German mystical tradition, we approach God through "unknowing" or "learned ignorance," through setting aside images, concepts, and propositions about God and purely experiencing his ineffable presence (Balthasar 1991a: 48–246). As on some Greek philosophies, images and material things here have only a didactic or preparatory role and are ultimately to be set aside. At times, these spiritualities can be in tension with sacramental spirituality and with the iconographic focus of the Second Council of Nicaea (Pfau 2022: 249–50).

One problem about God arising from the tension between cataphatic and apophatic approaches has to do with our knowledge of God. For some cataphatic approaches, especially those of the scholastic tradition, propositions can express literal truths about God, even though no proposition captures everything about God (*ST* I, q.13, a.3). They can even express, to some extent, *what* God is, in the sense of expressing which divine attribute explains all the others. For example, Thomists claim that God is *existence itself*. Since *existence*, on this view, means actuality or perfection as such and includes all other perfections, this divine attribute explains the other divine attributes (Garrigou-Lagrange 1938).

For many apophatic approaches, by contrast, directing one's attention away from material things, images, and concepts prepares the soul to perceive God's direct revelation of himself. In the Sacraments of Baptism and Confirmation, the Holy Spirit is understood to give us gifts and virtues that make us like God and able to readily act at his prompting; through ascetical and mystical practice, we become aware of God through an experience of intimate closeness to him made possible by these divine gifts. What is given in this experience cannot be imaginatively pictured or expressed propositionally. Thomas Aquinas calls this a knowledge of God "by connaturality," that is, by coming to have a nature like his (*ST* II–II, q.45, a.2). Others call this experience "spiritual sense" or "spiritual perception" (Gavrilyuk & Coakley 2012). But there have been tensions over how to understand the Spirit's gifts. On the approach of some *charismatic* movements, a major spirituality in contemporary Catholicism, one grasps and ought to attend to distinct revelations given by the Spirit, which reveal who God is (Walsh 1974). On more mystical approaches, by contrast, one is supposed to not attend to apparent revelations but direct one's attention away from gifts toward the giver of those gifts, who is never grasped cataphatically. If a gift is from God, it will have a positive effect, regardless of whether one attends to it (John of the Cross 1991: 263–4). Some mystical spiritualities are clearly in tension with the incarnational, sacramental aspects of Catholicism, aiming at a non-bodily, interior, private, and inexpressible perceptual experience of God. Others just seek to purify our images and concepts, allowing some use of imagery (like nuptial imagery) for divine union, admitting the need for liturgy and doctrine to guide experience, and emphasizing charitable service to others.

Despite these allowances, there is still a tension in Catholic spirituality between approaches on which God is made known by physical things accessible through ordinary experience and approaches on which he entirely transcends physical things and is accessible only by setting aside ordinary experience (Cooper 2014). On the former, our union with God involves bodily acts; on the latter, despite the incarnation being a permanent feature of God, we only attain full union with God by moving beyond attention to anything material. The question is whether we can ultimately move beyond the "scandal" of the incarnation – the shocking, unanticipatable experience of God being uniquely and definitively manifested in a particular bodily man and a particular institution – to an experience of God in himself, abstractly, and beyond all his manifestations (Balthasar 1990b). The most fruitful approaches have resolved this tension through accounts that capture both experiences and allow us to conceive of God as both present in and transcending material particulars. The idea that both approaches ought to be included in a Catholic conception of God is expressed in the liturgy, where we ask for aid to love God "in all things and above all things" and thereby achieve both what God has promised – what we can expect to achieve – and also what exceeds every desire (Roman Missal, Collect for the Fifth Sunday after Pentecost). I next turn to the *analogy of being*, which allows us to accomplish this goal of articulating a conception of God that includes all of these aspects.

4.4 Analogies of Being

We have seen that, on most Catholic views, we can reason from the existence of creatures to the existence of God. On that basis, God is understood as the supreme being or as being itself. The question then arises whether "being" means the same thing when predicated of God and of creatures (and the same question can be asked about other terms applied to both, like "good," "merciful," "powerful," and so forth). One approach, developed by the Church Father who called himself Dionysius and later by St. Thomas Aquinas, is called the "three-fold way" (*triplex via*) (Pseudo-Dionysius 1987: 135–41; Aquinas 1950; *ST* I, q.12–13). This "way" is both an account of how knowledge of God and language about God ought to develop, and an account of stages in the spiritual life.

We generally begin the ascent to knowledge of, or union with, God cataphatically, holding that just as creatures are beings, good, and so forth, so is God the cause of all these properties in creatures and so can all these properties be affirmed of him. In the spiritual life, we begin by relating to God through material realities, as on the "sacramental" spiritualities. But then we note that God is not a being, good, or anything else in the same way that creatures are. For example, creatures are contingently beings, while God exists necessarily; creatures have their properties by composition, while God simply is all of his properties. We then deny all of the predicates previously applied to God, holding that God is not a being, not good, and so forth. In the spiritual life, we ascetically distance ourselves from material aids to approaching God and allow God to remove our attachment to these things, an experience often called the "dark night" (John of the Cross 1991: 113–21). Finally, we perceive that these properties are found in God "super-eminently" or "in a more excellent way" than how they are found in creatures. This is to grasp not only that we can make true claims about God but also that God exceeds what we understand by those claims. Having been purified, we are again able to experience God's presence in material things, while also experiencing God as transcending that presence. To grasp each step requires disciplining one's desires and knowledge such that one comes to *perceive* what is affirmed at that step. Still, the truths affirmed at the final step can be *grasped* by anyone through analogy, even if they can only be truly *experienced* after going through the first two steps. Catholics have conceived of God by analogy to creatures in at least two ways; problems about God in Catholicism include the question of which account of analogy captures how language about God should work and the question of whether an analogical model is the best account of such language.

First, there is the *analogy of attribution* (Wippel 2000: 543–72). A term is properly said of something (the "primary analogate"), and it is said in secondary senses of things related to the primary analogate as its cause, effect, or sign. For example, the term "healthy" is said primarily of healthy organisms and secondarily of things that cause or preserve health like good diet or exercise. Likewise, "good," "being," or other perfection terms are said primarily of God and secondarily of creatures insofar as they are effects and signs of, and participate in, God. On this analogy, only God is being, good, and so forth properly speaking, while other things are only beings or goods insofar as they are God's effects. The terms we have devised to pick out perfections in creatures like "being" and "good" refer properly only to God, to whose perfection we have no direct access. As a result, we do not properly understand these terms. This sense of analogy captures the feeling that we do *not* really understand what we mean when we speak of God. It also captures the views that the fundamental metaphysical distinction in reality is between God and creation, that all being and perfection resides in God, and that creatures do not "add" to the "sum total" of being or perfection in reality; rather, they are just reflections of God's being and perfection, an unfolding of what God is, with everything positive in them really and primarily existing in God (Sokolowski 1995). But one might object that creatures *are* beings in their own right and not merely effects of being properly speaking, that we do understand words like "being," that this view of analogy fits best with occasionalism or quietism, on which creatures' value or causal power entirely resides in God, and that it does not fit well with the fully Catholic conception of God and creatures.

Second, there is the *analogy of proper proportionality* (Hochschild 2010; Przywara 2014). Some terms (and the realities to which they refer) can only be understood by considering multiple, proportioned relations between properties and things. For example, to grasp the full concept of "seeing" and to grasp what *seeing* really is, we must grasp that sensory seeing is to the eye as intellectual seeing is to the mind. Each is a proper sense of "seeing," though the two are hierarchically arranged. Intellectual seeing is a more complete seeing of an object than sensory seeing is. But there are not different "amounts" of a univocal "seeing" in both instances. Rather, each is a distinct kind of seeing; each points beyond itself to the other, but neither is reducible to the other. Similarly, to grasp "being," we cannot grasp just one sort of being but must understand the similarity or proportion between how existence is found in creatures and how it is found in God. The lower, secondary proportion in the analogy, that between creatures and their existence, points to and partially reveals the higher, primary proportion. On this analogy, we know what our words mean; to grasp perfections in creatures is to grasp that they are analogically related to higher perfections, which we thereby partially grasp. This analogy captures the view that God and his perfections are not only in creatures but also transcendent to them.

On both views, our knowledge of and language about God are understood to be *realist and metaphysical*, that is, analogical *language* reflects the analogical or participatory *structure of reality*. Some have understood this relation aesthetically: we *perceive* the analogical structure of reality by seeing how creatures (especially by their beauty) point like images beyond themselves to God, who is essentially beauty and perfection (Balthasar 2000). But God has not only been conceived by analogy to creatures on the Catholic tradition. Some have understood claims about God, including doctrinal claims, to be only "grammatical" – that is, they tell us what we may say about God, but they do not necessarily give knowledge of what God is like in himself (Van Wert 2020). Such a view must avoid the danger of *modernism*, a view excluded by the Catholic magisterium, on which all claims about God are historically contingent, changeable symbols of deeper affective experiences of God. On any orthodox Catholic conception of God, there are definite propositions that are always true of God (D 3401–26, 3477–90).

Other Catholic thinkers emphasize the uniqueness of God's revelation in Christ such that terms applied to God on the basis of that revelation are understood in an *equivocal* or entirely different sense to how they are applied outside that revelation. On such views, the revelation of God in Christ requires us to radically revise our understanding of and terms for all things, as well as our entire moral and spiritual outlook (Girard 1987). Others have resisted the third stage of the *triplex via*, insisting on a purely negative theology, on which we cannot speak of God at all but can only approach him by feeling (Pfau 2022: 325–32). But these *fideisitic* tendencies are minority currents in the Catholic tradition, and they have generally been resisted: the Catholic tradition has insisted on our ability to know and speak definitively and propositionally of God, both by our natural rational abilities and by grace and revelation.

Still others hold that terms apply to God and creatures univocally, that is, in the same sense. John Duns Scotus argued that we can abstract from the analogically related *metaphysical* differences between God and creatures and form a *concept* of being and other perfections that applies to both God and creatures. If by the word "being" we mean "not nothing," then "being" is said in that same sense of God and creatures. If we can reason from creatures to God, we must be able to form and use such univocal concepts, on pain of committing the fallacy of equivocation, and so invalidating that reasoning (Cross 2005). This does not mean that real, metaphysical being itself is the same in God and creatures; rather, it is only our concept and term "being" that are predicated univocally of God and creatures. Yet, to hold this view risks coming to think that being itself *does* have the same metaphysical nature in God and creatures or of coming to think of being as a real category that is prior to and explanatory of God (Balthasar 1991: 16–29). Catholic conceptions of God emerge from the tension between seeing God as transcendent to all conceivable beings and grasping God and creatures as both genuine beings.

4.5 Realist and Transcendentalist Routes to God

We saw in Section 3 how the work of St. Thomas Aquinas came to dominate Western Catholic thinking, especially beginning in the late nineteenth century. His philosophy was seen as an answer to strands of modern philosophy stemming from Immanuel Kant (1724–1804), on which, due to the structure of human knowledge, we cannot directly know reality itself or reason causally about reality as a whole and, thus, cannot directly prove or rationally know that God exists. Thomism, by contrast, is a realist philosophy: we grasp reality because knowing involves receiving forms from beings; since forms are the cause in beings whereby they have their identity, reception of a being's form conforms our mind to that being, enabling us to know it as it is. Our minds are naturally oriented to grasp beings and then ask why they exist – that is, to inquire into their causes. We have an innate, natural desire – a teleological orientation that results from our nature and is felt as a longing – to know beings and grasp their causes. Our minds are naturally oriented to reason to the existence of God, the first cause (Maritain 1995).

Since the modern Thomistic movement began in the late nineteenth century, Catholic thinkers have debated *how* our nature is oriented to union with God, that is, *how* we naturally desire God; this is also a debate over how God should be conceived in relation to us. It has often been a debate both over how to interpret St. Thomas and over what the truth is about these issues. This debate over how we desire God is related to the debate over how God is knowable, which was discussed earlier. It is also a debate about *how* and *in what ways* God is made present through creatures, which, as we have seen, is central to Catholic conceptions of God.

A first side of this debate came from the Dominican and Jesuit traditions (Feingold 2004). On this view, God has given all creatures natures, internal causes that make them belong to some kind and that reflect God's perfections in a definite way. Natures orient creatures to perform actions, whereby those creatures can achieve goods that fulfill them. When acting in virtue of their nature, creatures can achieve these goods under their own power without aid from God other than his general concurrence with creaturely actions. The goods to which a nature orients a creature are *proportioned* to that creature – that is, they are on the same metaphysical level of perfection as that creature, and so the creature can achieve those goods by individual or social effort. But no creature is proportioned to God in himself since God is infinite while creatures are finite. So, we can only have a natural desire to know God insofar as he can be known through our own effort, not as he is in himself. On this view, we naturally desire to know God as first cause of creatures. To know or desire God in himself requires him to reveal himself and to act upon us such that we share in his life and his activity of self-knowledge. Supernatural life or grace raises our nature to a level of perfection we could never achieve on our own. We can receive grace because the human mind is a power that, in principle, can receive any being, but without grace, we cannot directly desire union with God in himself. Apart from grace and by our natural powers alone, we can at most say conditionally that we *would* desire to know God in himself were it possible, though under those conditions it is not. In Christ, God has given us the possibility of a life of deification that entirely exceeds nature.

God is conceived here as relating to, and made present in, the world in two ways: naturally, where he causes creatures to exist and reflect his perfections, and supernaturally, where he causes persons to participate in his life. Both are a gift; neither is earned or a "right": despite reflecting his perfections, nature has no claim upon God. Only those who have received grace or participation in God's life, which ordinarily comes through the Sacraments (though God can give it in other ways), achieve eternal life with God. Everyone who does not receive grace, including those who only have natural knowledge of God, regardless of their moral state, will be eternally separated from God in himself. Some such persons may be in "limbo," a state of natural happiness and contemplation of God as first cause; others will be in "hell," a state of total separation from God (*ST* Supp., q.69). On this view, neither natural nor supernatural desire for God are purely internal, felt states; they must be lived out in one's concrete actions. To be good persons, our actions must consciously be done for the sake of God. To knowingly and with free, deliberate consent perform an action such that something other than God is one's ultimate end in doing it (that is, to commit a "mortal sin") is to cease to share in his life (*ST* I–II, q.88).

The way in which we conceive of God in relation to us and as desired by us affects all aspects of how we live out our relations to him because each such conception fits best with some account of Christian life and practices. Evangelization, telling others about Christ and the life of grace, is necessary on the view that I just described in order to bring people to the possibility of perfect happiness. While non-Judeo-Christian cultures can have aspects that anticipate grace – like an awareness that God exists and that we ought to worship him – such cultures are not all anticipations of Christianity. God is not present in all human actions, desires, or ways of life; he is only present through nature itself and through grace. This view is, in part, responsible for the great efforts at evangelization during the last five centuries. On this view, God need not give gifts to all people, and he is conceived as ordinarily giving gifts through the human mediation of evangelization, Sacraments, and the Catholic Church. Furthermore, since all of God's gifts are gratuitous, he can give greater gifts to some people. This view fits with a strong view of the Church's hierarchy: God gives greater participation in his authority and knowledge to priests and bishops or to spiritual directors than to others, and so they ought to be obeyed as making present the authority of God. This hierarchical, vertical notion of God's relation to Christians is reflected, for example, in liturgies focused on the priest's sacrificial actions. God's absolute call to goodness is conceived here as made present through concrete moral norms and human authorities.

A contrasting set of views is sometimes called the "new theology" (*nouvelle théologie*) by contrast to older versions of Thomism (Garrigou-Lagrange 1946) or the "*ressourcement*" movement because these views aimed to return to the sources of Catholic thought, such as the Fathers of the Church. It also sought a greater rapprochement with modern philosophy. Though, like the older view, many versions of this view are *realist* about our knowledge of things, this view is also *transcendentalist*: following Kant, it reflects on what the conditions in us are that allow us to have experiences at all. Prior to all knowledge, this view claims that we have an innate desire for knowledge of and union with the ultimate cause of things; we could not know or desire any being *as being* or any good *as good*, except on the basis of an implicit awareness of and desire for *being and goodness as such*. But "being itself" just is God in himself, and so we have an innate desire for God in himself. The very structure of intentional knowing and willing is seen here as revealing the existence of God (Purcell 2006: 112–22; Hart 2013).

This view was influenced by personalism, which introduced a key debate over how God is to be conceived and how we ought to relate to him. On the Thomistic view, God is conceived as *good*, that is, as desirable and fulfilling to us. God is not a means to our fulfillment but rather is to be loved for his own sake with reference to our fulfillment. God is our creator, and we owe him a grateful return for our existence. He is also goodness itself and so is due all the desire and love elicited by any good, all of which participate in him (*ST* I, q.6; II–II, q.81–82). God, on this view, is a "common good," that is, a good that can be shared by many participants and that is desirable precisely insofar as it is sharable. All things in the cosmos share in God's goodness by participating in him for their perfections, but created persons can share in him through deification and becoming members of his body, the Church. God is also an "honorable" or "beautiful" good (*bonum honestum*), one whose fulfilling benefits only come when desired for his own sake (Waldstein 2015). But the personalists object to the Thomists that God is not only a good in the sense of an object of *desire*. God is *important in himself*, such that we owe him awe, reverence, and total commitment, regardless of whether he fulfills us; we should not always approach him with reference to our fulfillment, as would be the case if we only approached him through desire. The personalist stance is manifested in the liturgy, when we pray "we give you thanks for your great glory" (Roman Missal, Gloria), that is, we thank him for the beauty and goodness he is in himself. God is not just one in whom we participate but one before whom we stand in dialogue, one who calls for and deserves total commitment of life (Hildebrand 2016).

On a version of *nouvelle théologie* promoted by Henri de Lubac and other members of what is called the *Communio* school of theology, human beings *by nature* desire grace and union with God in himself. We naturally reach beyond what we can achieve by our own efforts to seek gifts from others – that is, as on the personalist view, we enter a dramatic dialogue of gift and receptivity with other persons. This does not make those gifts earned. Rather, we can only be naturally fulfilled if God gives us the unearned gift of grace. As beings who can know *any* being and desire *any* good, we are naturally oriented to union with God. But God must give us the grace necessary to achieve this goal, and he did that through Christ. Yet, he gave us the orientation to that goal (and thereby, implicitly, the promise to give the aid) in our very creation. Every human act is performed on the basis of this natural desire; every human act carries something of grace, even if we can, in sin, also take something other than God as an ultimate end (de Lubac 1946 and 1998b).

On another version of this view, Karl Rahner and other members of what is called the *Concilium* school of theology held, like traditional Thomists, that there is a distinction between our nature and its desires and our orientation to grace. But every human being is given the supernatural gift of an orientation to grace; indeed, on this view, grace is operative in every human being from the beginning of their lives, though we can reject grace and the orientation to it. At all times, we have an implicit knowledge of and desire for being and goodness themselves, that is, God. Desires for particular goods and knowledge of particular beings are always had within the context of that general knowledge and desire. Grace arises out of what appears to be entirely natural since God intended all of nature, especially human nature, to be the site of his self-revelation (Rahner 1978: 120–8).

On either version of the *nouvelle théologie*, we cannot but desire God, though we can also oppose this innate desire. On de Lubac's view, nature could be seen as "supernaturalized": everything is grace, the communication of God's deifying gifts. One worry about this view is that it compromises God's gratuity in deifying us: If we have a natural desire for God in himself, and if natural desires are proportioned to their objects, then our natures seem to be proportioned to God in himself; our nature might then be seen as intrinsically supernatural or divine, such that receiving God's life belongs to us by nature, not by a special gift. This could be understood in a way contrary to the distinction between God and creatures that has been a hallmark of most Catholic conceptions (Feingold 2004: 414–16). On Rahner's view, grace could be seen as "naturalized": even the most everyday actions manifest God's gift of desire and revelation, and all actions reach beyond themselves toward God. Here, to accept human existence just is to accept God's self-revelation and grace. It is thereby possible for persons who have never heard about Christ to nevertheless be living a Christian life, a life of charity and deification, albeit "anonymously." This view tends to focus more on the basic orientation of one's life for or against grace – the personal commitment of life one makes in response to God's call – than on particular sins or moral norms (Rahner 1978: 398–411; Cooper 2014). It tends to promote a view of liturgy that is less hierarchical or vertically focused on encountering God through transcendent acts and that is more horizontal, focused on encountering God in other human persons. As in the Greek tradition and in some mystical spiritualities, God is here conceived as calling us to goodness in a way transcending particular, contingent manifestations of that goodness. A worry about this view is that it downplays the seriousness of explicit, concrete Christian commitment to God, making nearly any way of life good enough to attain union with God; God then is no longer conceived as made present through definite choices and actions, as calling for a definite response, and his orientation to concrete mediation is compromised (Balthasar 1994a). On both newer views, and unlike many older views, aspects of all human cultures reveal God and our orientation to him. Given the general orientation of human life toward God, they emphasize God's universal will to save and deify persons and, unlike on traditional Catholic views, argue that we should confidently hope that all persons will reach this ultimate end. The purpose of evangelization here is to bring persons to explicitly become aware of God's saving and deifying work in our lives, and thereby live a life of greater flourishing, virtue, and service to others.

The current tensions in the Catholic Church over liturgy, doctrine, evangelization, and morality are, in part, a consequence of the fact that each of these views on our desire for God has major proponents in the Church today. Many (including me) think that some hybrid of these views is preferable, for example, retaining from the older view the vertical emphasis on the greatness of God and its expression in liturgy, and the distinction of nature and supernature, while affirming the awareness of the newer views that each human culture and ordinary life reveal and orient us toward God. But in any case, these debates show the range of conceptions of God possible on a Catholic view and the problems regarding God to which they can lead. I hope that the tension between these views will bear fruit not only in a truer and more complete Catholic conception of God but also in an increased participation in the life of the God "in whom we live and move and have our being" (*Acts* 17:28).

Abbreviations

CCC	*Catechism of the Catholic Church*
D	Denzinger, *Compendium of Creeds, Definitions, and Declarations on Matters of Faith and Morals*, followed by paragraph number
ST	Thomas Aquinas, *Summa theologiae*

References

Anselm of Canterbury (1998). *The Major Works*, Brian Davies and Gillian R. Evans, eds., Oxford: Oxford University Press.

Aquinas, Thomas (2011). *Opera omnia*, Navarre: Fundación Tomás de Aquino. [All citations in the following Aquinas sources drawn from www.corpusthomisticum.org.]

Aquinas, Thomas (1856). *Scriptum super Sententiis*, Parma: Petrus Fiaccadori.

Aquinas, Thomas (1888–1906). *Summa theologiae*, Rome: S. C. de Propaganda Fide.

Aquinas, Thomas (1950). *In librum Beati Dionysii De divinis nominibus expositio*, Turin: Marietti.

Aquinas, Thomas (1954a). *Expositio libri Boetii De ebdomadibus*, Turin: Marietti.

Aquinas, Thomas (1954b). *Commentaria in octo libros Physicorum*, Turin: Marietti.

Aquinas, Thomas (1961). *Summa contra gentiles*, Turin: Marietti.

Aquinas, Thomas (1972). *De principiis naturae*, Rome: Santa Sabina.

Athanasius (1996). *On the Incarnation*, Crestwood: St. Vladimir's Seminary Press.

Augustine (1887a). On Baptism, Against the Donatists. In Philip Schaff, ed., and John R. King, trans., *Nicene and Post-Nicene Fathers*, vol. 4, (pp. 411–514), Buffalo: Christian Literature. https://newadvent.org/fathers.

Augustine (1887b). On the Predestination of the Saints. In Philip Schaff and Henry Wace, eds., and Peter Holmes and Robert Ernest Wallis, trans., *Nicene and Post-Nicene Fathers*, vol. 5, (493–520), Buffalo: Christian Literature. https://newadvent.org/fathers.

Augustine (1991). *Confessions*, Henry Chadwick, trans., Oxford: Oxford University Press.

Augustine (1992). *Sermons 148–183*, Edmund Hill, trans., New Rochelle: New City Press.

Augustine (2002). *On the Trinity*, Stephen McKenna, trans., Cambridge: Cambridge University Press.

Austriaco, Nicanor, James Brent, Thomas Davenport, and John Baptist Ku (2019). *Thomistic Evolution*, Providence: Cluny Media.

Ayers, Lewis (2006). *Nicaea and Its Legacy: An Approach to Fourth-Century Trinitarian Theology*, Oxford: Oxford University Press.

Balthasar, Hans Urs von (1987). *Truth Is Symphonic*, Graham Harrison, trans., San Francisco: Ignatius Press.

Balthasar, Hans Urs von (1989). *The Glory of the Lord*, vol. 4, *The Realm of Metaphysics in Antiquity*, Brian McNeil, Andrew Louth, John Saward, Rowan Williams, and Oliver Davies, trans., San Francisco: Ignatius Press.

Balthasar, Hans Urs von (1990a). *Theo-Drama*, vol. 2, *Dramatis Personae: Man in God*, Graham Harrison, trans., San Francisco: Ignatius Press.

Balthasar, Hans Urs von (1990b). *The Scandal of the Incarnation*, John Saward, trans., San Francisco: Ignatius Press.

Balthasar, Hans Urs von (1991a). *The Glory of the Lord*, vol. 5, *The Realm of Metaphysics in the Modern Age*, Oliver Davies, Andrew Louth, Brian McNeil, John Saward, and Rowan Williams, trans., San Francisco: Ignatius Press.

Balthasar, Hans Urs von (1991b). *The Glory of the Lord*, vol. 6, *Theology: The Old Covenant*, Brian McNeil and Erasmo Leiva-Merikakis, trans., San Francisco: Ignatius Press.

Balthasar, Hans Urs von (1992). *Theo-Drama*, vol. 3, *Dramatis Personae: Persons in Christ*, Graham Harrison, trans., San Francisco: Ignatius Press.

Balthasar, Hans Urs von (1994a). *The Moment of Christian Witness*, Richard Beckley, trans., San Francisco: Ignatius Press.

Balthasar, Hans Urs von (1994b). *Theo-Drama*, vol. 4, *The Action*, Graham Harrison, trans., San Francisco: Ignatius Press.

Balthasar, Hans Urs von (1998). *Theo-Drama*, vol. 5, *The Last Act*, Graham Harrison, trans., San Francisco: Ignatius Press.

Balthasar, Hans Urs von (2000). *Theo-Logic*, vol. 1, *Truth of the World*, Adrian Walker, trans., San Francisco: Ignatius Press.

Balthasar, Hans Urs von (2004). *Theo-Logic*, vol. 2, *Truth of God*, Adrian Walker, trans., San Francisco: Ignatius Press.

Balthasar, Hans Urs von (2005). *Theo-Logic*, vol. 3, *The Spirit of Truth*, Graham Harrison, trans., San Francisco: Ignatius Press.

Balthasar, Hans Urs von (2009). *The Glory of the Lord*, vol. 1, *Seeing the Form*, Erasmo Leiva-Merikakis, trans., San Francisco: Ignatius Press.

Bañez, Domingo (1585). *Scholastica commentaria in primam partem*, Salamanca: Apud S. Stephanum.

Basil the Great (1980). *On the Holy Spirit*, Crestwood: St. Vladimir's Seminary Press.

Benedict XVI (Josef Ratzinger) (2004). *Introduction to Christianity*, J. R. Foster, trans., San Francisco: Ignatius Press.

Benedict XVI (2005). *Deus caritas est*, Encyclical Letter, Vatican City.

Benedict XVI (2006). *Faith, Reason and the University: Memories and Reflections*, Papal Lecture, Vatican City.

Benedict XVI (2007). *Spe salvi*, Encyclical Letter, Vatican City.

Bernard of Clairvaux (1971–1980). *Sermons on the Song of Songs*, 4 vols., Kilian Walsh, trans., Collegeville: Cistercian.

Bonaventure (1882). *Commentaria in quatuor libros Sententiarum*, Quaracchi: Collegium S. Bonaventurae.

Bradshaw, David (2007). *Aristotle East and West*, Cambridge: Cambridge University Press.

Brown, Peter (2000). *Augustine of Hippo: A Biography*, Berkeley: University of California Press.

Cano, Melchior (1563). *De locis theologicis*, Salamanca: Mathias Gastius.

Interdicasterial Commission for the Catechism of the Catholic Church (1994). *Catechism of the Catholic Church*, New York: Doubleday.

Chesterton, Gilbert K. (2001). *Orthodoxy*, Colorado Springs: Shaw Books.

Clarke, Norris (1993). *Person and Being*, Milwaukee: Marquette University Press.

Clarke, Norris (1994). *Explorations in Metaphysics*, Notre Dame: University of Notre Dame Press.

Cooper, Adam G. (2014). *Naturally Human, Supernaturally God*, Minneapolis: Fortress Press.

Congregation for the Doctrine of the Faith (1984). *Instruction on Certain Aspects of the "Theology of Liberation,"* Vatican City. www.vatican.va/roman_curia/congregations/cfaith/documents/rc_con_cfaith_doc_19840806_theology-liberation_en.html.

Costello, Damian (2005). *Black Elk: Colonialism and Lakota Catholicism*, Maryknoll: Orbis.

Cousins, Ewert (1978). *Bonaventure and the Coincidence of Opposites*, Chicago: Franciscan Herald Press.

Crosby, John (1996). *The Selfhood of the Human Person*, Washington, DC: Catholic University of America Press.

Cross, Richard (2005). *Duns Scotus on God*, London: Routledge.

Damascene, John (1899). An Exposition of the Orthodox Faith. In Philip Schaff and Henry Wace, eds., and Stewart D. F. Salmond, trans., *Nicene and Post-Nicene Fathers*, vol. 9, (pp. 1–101), Buffalo: Christian Literature. https://newadvent.org/fathers.

Davies, Brian (2004). *An Introduction to the Philosophy of Religion*, Oxford: Oxford University Press.

Dean, Maximillian Mary (2006). *A Primer on the Absolute Primacy of Christ*, New Bedford: Academy of the Immaculate.

de Caussade, Jean-Pierre (2010). *Abandonment to Divine Providence*, E. J. Strickland, trans., Charlotte: Tan.

de Koninck, Charles (2009). Ego Sapientia: The Wisdom That Is Mary. In Ralph McInerny, trans., *The Writings of Charles de Koninck*, vol. 2, (pp.4–62), Notre Dame: University of Notre Dame Press.

de Lubac, Henri (1946). *Surnaturel*, Paris: Aubier.

de Lubac, Henri (1998a). *Medieval Exegesis*, vol. 1, *The Four Senses of Scripture*, Mark Sebanc, trans., Grand Rapids: Eerdmans.

de Lubac, Henri (1998b). *The Mystery of the Supernatural*, Rosemary Sheed, trans., New York: Crossroad.

de Lubac, Henri (1999). *The Splendor of the Church*, Michael Mason, trans., San Francisco: Ignatius Press.

de Molina, Luis (1595). *Liberi arbitrii cum gratiae donis, divina praescientia, providentia, praedestinatione, et reprobatione concordia*, Antwerp: Ioachimi Trognaesii.

Denzinger, Heinrich (2012). *Compendium of Creeds, Definitions, and Declarations on Matters of Faith and Morals*, Peter Hünermann, Robert Fastiggi, and Anne Englund Nash, eds., San Francisco: Ignatius Press.

de Sales, Francis (1997). *Treatise on the Love of God*, Henry Benedict Mackey, trans., Charlotte: Tan.

Dumont, Stephen (2005). Duns Scotus' Parisian Question on the Formal Distinction. *Vivarium* 43: 7–62.

Emery, Gille (2010). *The Trinitarian Theology of St. Thomas Aquinas*, Francesca Aran Murphy, trans., Oxford: Oxford University Press.

Fagerberg, David W. (2021). *Liturgical Dogmatics: How Catholic Beliefs Flow from Liturgical Prayer*, San Francisco: Ignatius Press.

Farges, Albert (1926). *Mystical Phenomena*, S. P. Jacques, trans., New York: Benzinger.

Feingold, Lawrence (2004). *The Natural Desire to See God according to St. Thomas Aquinas and His Interpreters*, Ave Maria: Sapientia Press.

Feingold, Lawrence (2021). *Touched by Christ: The Sacramental Economy*, Steubenville: Emmaus Academic.

Francis (2015). *Laudato Si'*, Encyclical Letter, Vatican City.

Freddoso, Alfred (1994). God's General Concurrence with Secondary Causes: Pitfalls and Prospects. *American Catholic Philosophical Quarterly* 68: 131–56.

Frost, Gloria (2014). Peter Olivi's Rejection of God's Concurrence with Created Causes. *British Journal for the History of Philosophy* 22: 655–79.

Garrigou-Lagrange, Reginald (1937). *Providence*, Bede Rose, trans., St. Louis: Herder.

Garrigou-Lagrange, Reginald (1938). *De deo uno*, Paris: Desclée de Brouwer et Cie.

Garrigou-Lagrange, Reginald (1946a). La nouvelle théologie où va-t-elle? *Angelicum* 23: 126–45.

Garrigou-Lagrange, Reginald (1946b). *Predestination*, Bede Rose, trans., St. Louis: Herder.

Garrigou-Lagrange, Reginald (2021). *Thomistic Common Sense: The Philosophy of Being and the Development of Doctrine*, Matthew Minerd, trans., Steubenville: Emmaus Academic.

Gavrilyuk, Paul and Sarah Coakley, eds. (2012). *The Spiritual Senses: Perceiving God in Western Christianity*, Cambridge: Cambridge University Press.

Germanus of St. Stanislaus (2000). *The Life of St. Gemma Galgani*, Charlotte: Tan.

Girard, René (1987). *Things Hidden Since the Foundation of the World*, Stephen Bann and Michael Metteer, trans., Stanford: Stanford University Press.

Gregory of Nazianzus (2002). *On God and Christ: The Five Theological Orations and Two Letters to Cledonius*, Frederick Williams and Lionel Wickahm, trans., Yonkers: St. Vladimir's Seminary Press.

Gregory of Nyssa (1893). Dogmatic Treatises. In Philip Schaff and Henry Wace, eds., and Henry A. Wilson and William More, trans., *Nicene and Post-Nicene Fathers, Second Series*, vol. 5, (pp. 33–342), Buffalo: Christian Literature. https://newadvent.org/fathers.

Gutiérrez, Gustavo (1988). *A Theology of Liberation: History, Politics, and Salvation*, Caridad Inda and John Eagleson, trans., Maryknoll: Orbis.

Hankey, Wayne J. (2019). Divine Henads and Persons: Multiplicity's Birth in the Principle in Proclus and Aquinas. *Dionysius* 37: 165–82.

Hart, David Bentley (2003). *The Beauty of the Infinite: The Aesthetics of Christian Truth*, Grand Rapids: Eerdmans.

Hart, David Bentley (2013). *The Experience of God: Being, Consciousness, Bliss*, New Haven: Yale University Press.

Hildebrand, Dietrich von (2016). *Liturgy and Personality*, Steubenville: Hildebrand Project.

Hildebrand, Dietrich von (2017). *In Defense of Purity*, Steubenville: Hildebrand Press.

Hipp, Stephen (2012). *The Doctrine of Personal Subsistence: Historical and Systematic Synthesis*, Fribourg: Studia Friburgensia.

Hochschild, Joshua (2010). *The Semantics of Analogy: Rereading Cajetan's De Nominium Analogia*, Notre Dame: University of Notre Dame Press.

Hoffman, Tobias (2013). Freedom Beyond Practical Reason: Duns Scotus on Will-Dependent Relations. *British Journal for the History of Philosophy* 21: 1071–90.

Hoffmann, Tobias and Cyrille Michon (2017). Aquinas on Free Will and Intellectual Determinism. *Philosopher's Imprint* 17: 1–36.

Ignatius of Loyola (1999). *The Spiritual Exercises*, Charlotte: Tan.

John of the Cross (1991). *Collected Works*, Kieran Kavanaugh and Otilio Rodriguez, trans., Washington, DC: ICS.

John Paul II (Karol Wojtyła) (1981a). *Love and Responsibility*, Harry T. Willetts, trans., San Francisco: Ignatius Press.

John Paul II (1981b). *Laborem exercens*, Encyclical Letter, Vatican City.

John Paul II (1994). *Crossing the Threshold of Hope*, Jenny McPhee and Martha McPhee, trans., New York: Knopf.

John Paul II (2005). *Man and Woman He Created Them: A Theology of the Body*, Michael Waldstein, trans., Boston: Pauline.

Johnson, Luke Timothy (2015). *The Revelatory Body: Theology as Inductive Art*, Grand Rapids: Eerdmans.

Johnston, William (1970). *The Still Point: Reflections on Zen and Christian Mysticism*, New York: Harper&Row.

Joy, John (2017). *On the Ordinary and Extraordinary Magisterium from Joseph Kleutgen to the Second Vatican Council*, Fribourg: Aschendorff Verlag.

Keefe, Donald J. (1991). *Covenantal Theology: The Eucharistic Order of History*, Lanham: University Press of America.

Knox, Ronald (1994). *Enthusiasm: A Chapter in the History of Religion*, Notre Dame: University of Notre Dame Press.

Leo XIII (1879). *Aeterni Patris*, Encyclical Letter, Rome.

Loudovikos, Nikolaos (2019). *Analogical Identities: The Creation of the Christian Self*, Turnhout: Brepols.

Marion, Jean-Luc (1995). *God Without Being*, Thomas Carlson, trans., Chicago: University of Chicago Press.

Marion, Jean-Luc (2008). *The Erotic Phenomenon*, Stephen Lewis, trans., Chicago: University of Chicago Press.

Maritain, Jacques (1995). *The Degrees of Knowledge*, Gerald Phelan, trans., Notre Dame: University of Notre Dame Press.

Maximus the Confessor (2022). Opuscula 3, 6, and 7. In Mark DelCogliano, ed., and Jonathan L. Zecher, and Mark DelCogliano, trans., *The Cambridge Edition of Early Christian Writings*, vol. 4, (pp. 492–517), *Christ: Chalcedon and Beyond*, Cambridge: Cambridge University Press.

Meconi, David Vincent (2018). *The One Christ: St. Augustine's Theology of Deification*, Washington, DC: Catholic University of America Press.

Narcisse, Gilbert (1997). *Les Raisons de Dieu: Argument de Convenance Et Esthétique Théologique Selon Saint Thomas d'Aquin Et Hans Urs von Balthasar*, Fribourg: Editions Universitaires Fribourg Suisse.

Newman, John Henry (1994). *An Essay on the Development of Christian Doctrine*, Notre Dame: University of Notre Dame Press.

O'Neill, Taylor Patrick (2019). *Grace, Predestination, and the Permission of Sin: A Thomistic Analysis*, Washington, DC: Catholic University of America Press.

Palamas, Gregory (1983). *The Triads*, Nicholas Gendle, trans., Mahwah: Paulist Press.

Pascal, Blaise (2008). *Pensées and Other Writings*, Anthony Levi and Honor Levi, trans., Oxford: Oxford University Press.

Pawl, Timothy (2016). *In Defense of Conciliar Christology: A Philosophical Essay*, Oxford: Oxford University Press.

Pawl, Timothy (2019). *In Defense of Extended Conciliar Christology: A Philosophical Essay*, Oxford: Oxford University Press.

Pawl, Timothy (2020). Conciliar Trinitarianism, Divine Identity Claims, and Subordinationism. *TheoLogica* 4: 102–28.

Perl, Eric (2014). *Thinking Being: Introduction to Metaphysics in the Classical Tradition*, Leiden: Brill.

Perszyk, Ken, ed. (2012). *Molinism: The Contemporary Debate*, Oxford: Oxford University Press.

Pfau, Thomas (2022). *Incomprehensible Certainty: Metaphysics and Hermeneutics of the Image*, Notre Dame: University of Notre Dame Press.

Pinckaers, Servias (1995). *The Sources of Christian Ethics*, Mary Thomas Noble, trans., Washington, DC: Catholic University of America Press.

Pontifical Council for Promoting Christian Unity (1995). The Father as the Source of the Whole Trinity: The Procession of the Holy Spirit in Greek and Latin Traditions. *Catholic International* 5: 36–43.

Przywara, Erich (2014). *Analogia Entis: Metaphysics: Original Structure and Universal Rhythm*, John Betz and David Bentley Hart, trans., Grand Rapids: Eerdmans.

Pseudo-Dionysius (1987). *The Complete Works*, Colm Luibheid, trans., Mahwah: Paulist Press.

Purcell, Michael (2006). *Levinas and Theology*, Cambridge: Cambridge University Press.

Radde-Gallwitz, Andrew (2009). *Basil of Caesarea, Gregory of Nyssa, and the Transformation of Divine Simplicity*, Oxford: Oxford University Press.

Rahner, Hugo (2021). *Greek Myths and Christian Mystery*, Brian Battershaw, trans., Providence: Cluny.

Rahner, Karl (1978). *Foundations of Christian Faith: An Introduction to the Idea of Christianity*, William Dych, trans., New York: Crossroad.

Rausch, Thomas (2003). *Who is Jesus? An Introduction to Christology*, Collegeville: Liturgical Press.

Richard of St. Victor (1855). *De Trinitate*, Paris: J. P. Migne.

Scheeben, Matthias (1946). *Mysteries of Christianity*, Cyril Vollert, trans., St. Louis: Herder.

Schoeman, Roy (2003). *"Salvation Is from the Jews" (John 4:22): The Role of Judaism in Salvation History from Abraham to the Second Coming*, San Francisco: Ignatius.

Scotus, John Duns (1954). *Ordinatio, Book 1, Distinction 3*, Vatican City: Typis Vaticanis.

Scotus, John Duns (2006). *Ordinatio, Book 3, Distinctions 1–17*, Vatican City: Typis Vaticanis.

Scotus, John Duns (2007). *Ordinatio, Book 3, Distinctions 27–40*, Vatican City: Typis Vaticanis.

Sheen, Fulton J. (1952). *The World's First Love*, New York: McGraw-Hill.

Sokolowski, Robert (1995). *The God of Faith and Reason: Foundations of Christian Theology*, Washington, DC: Catholic University of America Press.

Spencer, Mark K. (2016). Divine Causality and Created Freedom: A Thomistic Personalist View. *Nova et Vetera* 14: 375–419.

Spencer, Mark K. (2017). The Flexibility of Divine Simplicity: Aquinas, Scotus, Palamas. *International Philosophical Quarterly* 57: 123–39.

Spencer, Mark K. (2018). Perceiving the Image of God in the Whole Human Person. *The Saint Anselm Journal* 13: 1–18.

Spencer, Mark K. (2022a). A Metaphysics of Blood Sacrifice. *Proceedings of the American Catholic Philosophical Association* 96, forthcoming.

Spencer, Mark K. (2022b). *The Irreducibility of the Human Person: A Catholic Synthesis*, Washington, DC: Catholic University of America Press.

Spencer, Mark K. (2022c). Classical Theism, Divine Beauty, and the Doctrine of the Trinity. In Rob Koons and Jonathan Fuqua, eds., *Classical Theism: New Essays on the Metaphysics of God*, (pp. 285–302), New York: Routledge.

Spencer, Mark K. and Walter Matthews Grant (2015). Activity, Identity, and God: A Tension in Aquinas and His Interpreters. *Studia Neoaristotelica* 12: 5–61.

Spezzano, Daria (2015). *The Glory of God's Grace: Deification According to St. Thomas Aquinas*, Naples: Sapientia Press.

Stein, Edith (2002). *Finite and Eternal Being*, Kurt Reinhardt, trans., Washington, DC: ICS.

Stump, Eleonore (2003). *Aquinas*, New York: Routledge.

Stump, Eleonore (2010). *Wandering in Darkness: Narrative and the Problem of Suffering*, Oxford: Oxford University Press.

Suárez, Francisco (1861). *Metaphysical Disputations 28–51*, Paris: Vivès.

Teresa of Avila (1989). *Interior Castle*, Edgar Allison Peers, trans., New York: Image.

Theodore the Studite (1981). *On the Holy Icons*, Catherine Roth, trans., Crestwood: St. Vladimir's Seminary Press.

Thérèse of Lisieux (2006). *The Story of a Soul*, Robert Edmondson, trans., Brewster: Paraclete Press.

Tracy, David (1981). *The Analogical Imagination: Christian Theology and the Culture of Pluralism*, New York: Crossroad.

Turek, Margaret M. (2022). *Atonement: Soundings in Biblical, Trinitarian, and Spiritual Theology*, San Francisco: Ignatius Press.

Van Wert, Thomas Adam (2020). *Neither Nature nor Grace: Aquinas, Barth, and Garrigou-Lagrange on the Epistemic Use of God's Effects*, Washington, DC: Catholic University of America Press.

Waldstein, Edmund (2015). The Good, the Highest Good, and the Common Good. *The Josias*. https://thejosias.com.

Waldstein, Michael (2021). *Glory of the Logos in the Flesh: St. John Paul's Theology of the Body*, Ave Maria: Sapientia Press.

Walsh, Vincent M. (1974). *A Key to Charismatic Renewal in the Catholic Church*, Wynnewood: Key of David.

White, Thomas Joseph (2015). *The Incarnate Lord: A Thomistic Study in Christology*, Washington, DC: Catholic University of America Press.

White, Thomas Joseph (2022). *The Trinity: On the Nature and Mystery of the One God*, Washington, DC: Catholic University of America Press.

Wiitala, Michael (2019). Every Happy Man is a God: Deification in Boethius. In Jared Ortiz, ed., *Deification in the Latin Patristic Tradition*, (pp. 231–252), Washington, DC: Catholic University of America Press.

William of Ockham (1981). *Quaestiones in librum secundum Sententiarum (Reportatio)*, St. Bonaventure: St. Bonaventure University Press.

Wippel, John (2000). *The Metaphysical Thought of Thomas Aquinas: From Finite Being to Uncreated Being*, Washington, DC: Catholic University of America Press.

Wolter, Alan (1997). *Duns Scotus on the Will and Morality*, Washington, DC: Catholic University of America Press.

Acknowledgments

I am grateful to Matthews Grant, Tim Pawl, Mike Sauter, and two anonymous referees for their comments on earlier drafts of this Element.

Cambridge Elements ≡

The Problems of God

Series Editor
Michael L. Peterson
Asbury Theological Seminary

Michael Peterson is Professor of Philosophy at Asbury Theological Seminary.
He is the author of *God and Evil* (Routledge); *Monotheism, Suffering, and Evil*
(Cambridge University Press); *With All Your Mind* (University of Notre Dame Press);
C. S. Lewis and the Christian Worldview (Oxford University Press); *Evil and the Christian
God* (Baker Book House); and *Philosophy of Education: Issues and Options* (Intervarsity
Press). He is co-author of *Reason and Religious Belief* (Oxford University Press);
Science, Evolution, and Religion: A Debate about Atheism and Theism (Oxford University
Press); and *Biology, Religion, and Philosophy* (Cambridge University Press). He is editor of
The Problem of Evil: Selected Readings (University of Notre Dame Press). He is co-editor of
Philosophy of Religion: Selected Readings (Oxford University Press) and *Contemporary
Debates in Philosophy of Religion* (Wiley-Blackwell). He served as General Editor of the
Blackwell monograph series Exploring Philosophy of Religion and is founding
Managing Editor of the journal *Faith and Philosophy*.

About the Series
This series explores problems related to God, such as the human quest for God or gods,
contemplation of God, and critique and rejection of God. Concise, authoritative
volumes in this series will reflect the methods of a variety of disciplines, including
philosophy of religion, theology, religious studies, and sociology.

Cambridge Elements ≡

The Problems of God

Elements in the Series

Divine Guidance: Moral Attraction in Action
Paul K. Moser

God, Salvation, and the Problem of Spacetime
Emily Qureshi-Hurst

Orthodoxy and Heresy
Steven Nemes

God and Political Theory
Tyler Dalton McNabb

Evolution and Christianity
Michael Ruse

Evil and Theodicy
Laura W. Ekstrom

Catholicism and the Problem of God
Mark K. Spencer

A full series listing is available at: www.cambridge.org/EPOG.

Printed in the United States
by Baker & Taylor Publisher Services